Pursuing the Mind and Will of Jesus Christ

James Perry

Pursuing the Mind and Will of Jesus Christ

ISBN 9781733454094

DEDICATION

Edwin Stuart Walker, III

This book is dedicated to one who throughout his lifetime has demonstrated his willingness and desire to pursue the mind and will of Jesus Christ. Ed graduated from Columbia Bible College (now Columbia International University) in Columbia, South Carolina. Shortly after graduation, he was united in marriage to Mary Lee Fry (who was also a graduate of CBC).

Ed and Mary Lee were involved in a Church Plant in Lexington, Virginia. While planting the church, they applied to and were accepted to be missionaries with West Indies Mission (now WORLDTEAM) to serve in Haiti. They conducted ministry in Aux Cayes (in Southwestern, Haiti) and Port Au Prince, Haiti for twenty-three years. Ed would later become the director and president of WORLDTEAM until his retirement. He has proven to be a missionary statesman and a Biblical apologist.

Ed has also been a personal encouragement to my wife (his sister-in-law) and me for more than sixty-five years. It has been a privilege to be not only family members but also fellow-servants of the Lord Jesus Christ.

Ed epitomizes what it means to Pursue The Mind and Will Of Jesus Christ in both life and ministry.

It is a privilege and honor to dedicate this book to Edwin Stuart Walker, III.

Table of Contents

PROLOGUE

What does it mean to pursue the mind and will of Jesus Christ? What did Jesus know, what did he think and what did he do during his life? The following chapters will illustrate these things for us. One thing we do know – to emulate Christ requires a lifetime commitment and pursuit.

Some of the foundational basics are found within the following instructions and guidelines:

Mind Renewal - Romans 12:1-2

> I appeal to you therefore…by the mercies of God, to present your bodies as a living sacrifice, holy and acceptable to God, which is your spiritual worship. Do not be conformed to this world, but be transformed by the renewal of your mind, that by testing you may discern what is the will of God, what is good and acceptable and perfect.

Transformation must be occurring if one is to advance in spiritual development and growth. It is the only way one can effectively pursue and attain the mind and will of Jesus Christ.

Power At Work - Ephesians 3:20-21 (ESV)

> Now to him who is able to do far more abundantly than all that we ask or think, according to the power at work within us, to him be glory in the church and in Christ

Jesus throughout all generations, forever and ever. Amen.

The power at work within the transformed follower of Jesus Christ will open the potential for knowing, realizing and believing that the Eternal God is able to act on one's behalf "more abundantly" beyond one's capacity when asking, thinking or imagining what God can and will do.

Divine Power and Precious Promises - Second Peter 1:3-4 (ESV)

> His divine power has granted to us all things that pertain to life and godliness, through the knowledge of him who called us to his own glory and excellence, which he has granted to us his precious and very great promises, so that through them you may become partakers of the divine nature, having escaped from the corruption that is in the world because of sinful desire.

The follower of Jesus Christ must be aware of the power of Jesus Christ that will accomplish God's will in and through one's life. To reassure one, there are the precious and great promises that will sustain one's walk of faith and ongoing pursuit of the mind and will of Jesus Christ. How many precious and great promises are there? More than anyone can imagine or accurately enumerate. Some have estimated the number to be anywhere from approximately 3,000 up to 8,000 promises. Regardless of "how many", every promise of God is covered in the words of Paul when he wrote to the Biblical believers in Second Corinthians 1:20 (NLT) – "For all of God's promises have been fulfilled in Jesus Christ with a resounding "Yes!" And through Christ, our "Amen" (which means "Yes") ascends to God for his glory."

Are you ready to pursue the mind and will of Jesus Christ? Are you ready to begin the journey of faith so you can be all that He wants you become - to know, think, and do as Jesus? May you be encouraged in your walk with the Lord so that you will avoid being faint-hearted by the unfolding developments in the culture. May you be enabled to say along with the Apostle Paul: "…But we have the mind of Christ" (First Corinthians 1:20 ESV). As you daily pursue the mind and will of Jesus Christ, may a song of your heart be –

Standing on the promises of Christ my King,
Through eternal ages let his praises ring;
Glory in the highest, I will shout and sing,
Standing on the promises of God.

Standing on the promises I cannot fall,
Listening every moment to the Spirit's call,
Resting in my Savior as my all in all,
Standing on the promises of God.

Chapter One - THOUGHTS AND WAYS

Regardless of where one believes he/she is in one's spiritual walk, growth and development, there needs to be the realization that the pursuit of the mind and will of God is always ongoing. The prophet's words in Isaiah 55:6-9 (ESV) tell us:

> Seek the LORD while he may be found; call upon him while he is near; let the wicked forsake his way, and the unrighteous man his thoughts; let him return to the LORD, that he may have compassion on him, and to our God, for he will abundantly pardon. For my thoughts are not your thoughts, neither are your ways my ways, declares the LORD. For as the heavens are higher than the earth, so are my ways higher than your ways and my thoughts than your thoughts.

It is sobering to realize that despite one's progress in the pursuit of the mind and will of Christ, the journey is much longer and the instructions are still needed. It is beneficial to note the instruction Paul continues to give to God's people. The Book of Philippians is a good illustration. What does Paul observe and instruct about the thoughts and ways of God? In Philippians 2:5, Paul reminds the Church Members at Philippi, "Have this mind among yourselves, which is yours in Christ Jesus..." He precedes this challenge with his observations of what they are to be and do as believers (Verses 2-4),

> Complete my joy by being of the same mind, having the same love, being in full accord and of one mind. Do nothing from selfish ambition or conceit, but in humility count others more significant than yourselves. Let each of you look not only to his own interests, but also to the interests of others.

A point that Paul is making is it's possible to become satisfied with that which one is becoming and has been doing. It's a trap that is too easy to step into for the unsuspecting or the matter-of-fact. In verses 14-15, he reminds us of the spiritual behavior that is to be apparent in one's life. There needs to be awareness and a conscious act to avoid grumbling and disputing. Why? Because God's people are living "in the midst of a crooked and twisted generation." Rather than stepping aside, or a worst case scenario – becoming like the crooked and twisted generation, the child of God is to "shine as light in the world." These words remind me of the Chorus most of us learned and sang as children –

> This little light of mine,
> I'm going to let it shine…
> Hide it under a bushel? No!
> I'm going to let it shine!

Paul goes on to share additional thoughts about one's personal life and spiritual growth in Philippians 4:8-9,

Whatever is true …honorable …just …pure …lovely …commendable, if there is any excellence, if there is anything worthy of praise, think about these things. What you have learned and received and heard and seen in me, practice these things, and the God of peace will be with you.

Paul is challenging the people to be an example to others just as he had been an example to them. He wants them to know that it is more important for them to walk the walk than it is to talk the talk. It is similar to a question posed by Jesus Christ to His disciples, John 13:12, "Do you understand what I have done for you?" In verse 15, He adds: "I have given you an example, that you also should do just as I have done for you."

Getting one's thoughts aligned with the Lord's and one's ways representing God's ways is not just taught but is caught by the defined and observable example. The teaching would have had limited impact if it had not coincided with the example that demonstrated what the instruction means. In part, it was captured and emphasized in the prayer of Francis of Assisi, "Lord, make me an instrument of your peace…where there is despair let me bring hope…where there is darkness, let me bring your light…"

It is to implement one's belief with appropriate action. The follower of Jesus Christ must avoid theories about God and His power. It will be far more effective for that power to be observable in one's actions and lifestyle. The commentary offered by those opposed to the message of the Apostles is recorded in Acts 4:13.

> Now when they saw the boldness of Peter and John, and perceived that they were uneducated, common men, they were astonished. And they recognized that they had been with Jesus.

Do people pause and take note about us that we are the representatives of Jesus Christ - that His thoughts, ways, mind and will have captivated each of us? May the song of our hearts and lives be:

> We rest on Thee, our Shield and our Defender;
> We go not forth alone against the foe;
> Strong in Thy strength, safe in Thy keeping tender.
> We rest on Thee, and in Thy Name we go.

> We go in faith, our own great weakness feeling,
> And needing more each day Thy grace to know:
> Yet from our hearts a song of triumph pealing;
> We rest on Thee, and in Thy Name we go.

Chapter Two - MIND RENEWAL

Rene Descarte (1596-1650) was a French Scientist, Mathematician and Philosopher. Among his several contributions was the formulation of the first modern version of mind-body dualism which led him into the area of the mind-body discordant problem. Part of his philosophical quandary emerged from this dualistic view. As a dualist, Rene Descarte opposed any theory that identified the mind with the brain (which was considered a physical mechanism). As a thinker, he developed a system (theory) of "methodical doubt" in which he found no correlation between apparent knowledge that was derived from any authority or the senses. He concluded that when he was thinking, he existed. Flowing out of this viewpoint was a dictum (Latin: Cogito, Ergo Sum), "I think, therefore I am."

If only he had a place in his mind and thought theories for the following where Paul expressed, Romans 12:1-2,

> I appeal to you by the mercies of God, to present your bodies as a living sacrifice, holy and acceptable to God, which is your spiritual worship. Do not be conformed to this world, but be transformed by the renewal of your mind, that by testing you may discern what is the will of God, what is good and acceptable and perfect.

The mind has a multiple and varied capacities. A "mind" has the ability to reason, think, feel, will, perceive, discern, etc. The New Oxford American Dictionary indicates that the mind is: "The element of a person that enables them to be aware of the world and their experiences to think and to feel; the faculty of consciousness and thought."

Paul knew and conveyed that a cultural and worldly approach in life would overwhelm one's ability to discipline one's mind and its ability to think correctly. The solution is the transformation of one's body, soul and spirit in a sacrificial way to God. Such an act and commitment will result in a renewed mind and a discernment that encompasses God and His will which is good, perfect and acceptable.

Jesus illustrated this truth during His earthly ministry via the parable of the seed and the sower (Mark 4:3-9). He asked His disciples whether or not they understood the parable. One application He wanted them to absorb is found in Mark 4:18-19,

> And others (seeds) are the ones sown among thorns. They are those who hear the word, but the cares of the world and the deceitfulness of riches and the desires for other things enter in and choke the word, and it proves unfruitful.

The only adequate alternative is the transformation that passes one from death unto eternal life and results in one's mind being renewed so that discernment will replace any doubt.

As John penned some of his thoughts to followers of Jesus Christ, he amplified the teaching of both Jesus Christ and the Apostle Paul.

> Do not love the world or the things in the world. If anyone loves the world, the love of the Father is not in him. For all that is in the world, the desires of the flesh and the desires of the eyes and pride of life is not from the Father but is from the world. And the world is passing away along with its desires, but whoever does the will of God abides forever. First John 2:15-17 (ESV)

John draws a distinction between one's love for the world versus one's love of the Father. Love of the world will set one out to satisfy the desire(s) of the mind, emotion and will. It will begin to gain control of one's desires of the flesh, eyes and lifestyle. It also ignores the command Jesus Christ referenced with an inquiring lawyer: "You shall love the Lord your God with all your heart and with all your soul and with all your strength and with all your mind…" Luke 10:27.

How is your mind? Is there conflict between your love of things common in the culture and world versus your love for the Father and His will for your life? Are you at a place where (when) you need to have your mind renewed by the transforming grace of God?

A hymn written in the early 1900s by Kate B. Wilkinson is a good focus for one's conscious commitment and desire, as well as a possible daily prayer for one's life.

May the mind of Christ, my Savior
Live in me from day to day;
By His love and power controlling
All I do and say.

May I run the race before me,
Strong and brave to face the foe,
Looking only unto Jesus
As I onward go.

Chapter Three - NO REGRETS

While watching a virtual worship service, the subject of "a verse for the New Year" was mentioned. The minister allowed that concept was foreign to him inasmuch as years ago he had chosen a lifetime verse. It was Colossians 3:23-24,

> Whatever you do, work heartily, as for the Lord and not for men, knowing that from the Lord you will receive the inheritance as your reward. You are serving the Lord Christ.

All would acknowledge that these words were well-chosen and an awareness that should govern one's life.

Early in our courtship and marriage, my bride to be and I decided on verses that we would embrace for our lives and our family. We decided we would not purposely allow circumstances to be a factor that would divert our attention from the perfect will of God for our lives. As we approached marriage, two of the verses chosen were:

> Isaiah 65:24 (NIV), "Before they call I will answer; while they are still speaking I will hear."

> Hebrews 12:2, "Keep on looking to Jesus, the Author and Finisher of our faith."

> Little did we realize all of what that would include.

One situation occurred in our fifth year of marriage. Our third child had been conceived and we were looking forward to the child's birth. God had other plans. The baby was born prematurely. It was a son. We never got to see him – never got to hold him – never able to express our love to and for him. He lived a little more than 3 hours and then we were told that he had died.

Were we ready for that news? No! Did we have any regrets about not holding our son? Yes! Were we sad and disappointed in that news? Yes! What made that news bearable is that we had committed the infant to the Lord before any of the negative news was given. The words of Scripture became more real to us. Jeremiah 29:11, The Lord has perfect plans in place for us and our infant son; and Isaiah 26:3, "He will keep us in His perfect peace for those whose minds are steadfast, because they trust in you."

In the NLT, Isaiah 65:24 indicates: "While they are still talking about their needs, I will go ahead and answer their prayers!" Do we still have personal concerns? Yes! Do we continue to trust Him with no regrets? Yes! Do we still have particular needs? Yes! Are we as confident today as we were in our courtship that God cares and will provide for what our personal needs? Yes! We believe Philippians 4:19 (NIV), "Our God will meet all our needs according to the riches of His glory in Christ Jesus." The NLT has this phrase: "God who takes care of us will provide…" Will there be times when our "wants" become our expression to the Lord of what we believe we "need"? Yes! But He knows our heart and commitment. He will continue to fit us into His plan(s) for us.

It is vital that each of us remembers to be thankful. God never makes any mistakes. He knows the pathway laid out before us and will grant us safety and provision as we obediently walk in His way for us. A truth my wife and I cherish: God knows the way through the wilderness, All we have to do is follow...

When we were undergraduate students, a chorus that was often sung in chapel kept our commitment and priorities in focus:

I have decided to follow Jesus...
No turning back...

The Cross before me,
The world behind me...
No turning back...

The question that is always with one is how to get both thought and mind on Jesus Christ and His will. Many years ago, I heard a testimony about a track and field athlete. His feature event was the high jump. However, he seemed maxed out at one height. His desire was to raise the height of the bar. When that was done, he failed to clear it. Frustrated and dejected, he outwardly stated his disappointment and failure. He expressed: I can't clear the bar! How can I ever successfully get over the raised height. A nearby coach, a Biblical Christian, overheard the young man and came to him with a word of encouragement and guidance. He simply stated that if he threw his heart over the bar, the rest of his body would follow. That word resonated with the young athlete. In a future high jump, he easily cleared the bar. He was asked how he had finally succeeded after so many failures. His answer was: I threw my heart over the bar and I was able to clear it.

What does the Lord want from you and me in terms of our thinking His thoughts and knowing His mind? The school my bride and I attended had a motto: "To know Him and to make Him known." We believed that was to be our commitment and life choice. It would require one additional factor to accomplish that goal. For the athlete and for us, it involved a heart commitment. There is a refrain in an invitation hymn that expresses that which Jesus wants: Give Me thy heart, give me thy heart; O weary, wandering child, give Me thy heart.

Additionally, for us, it entailed another commitment. We agreed before the Lord that we would go anywhere, at any time, to do any work, at any cost. We have known each other and been together sixty-seven years and have never regretted that commitment and life choice.

It must also be remembered that as and when we recall these truths, our hearts should overflow with thanksgiving and gratitude to the Lord. We have never embraced any regrets. We have tried to remain focused on the faithfulness of our Lord. Psalm 100:4-5 reminds us to:

Enter his gates with thanksgiving; go into his courts with praise. Give thanks to him and praise his name. For the LORD is good. His unfailing love continues forever, and his faithfulness continues to each generation.

Chapter Four - SHELF LIFE

Each of us walks a fine line with the Lord when our desire is to pursue His thought, mind and will. Just like the athlete from the previous chapter, there is always the potential for discouragement in the pursuit of the goal of becoming Christ like. However, it doesn't have to be either fatal or final. Staying positive is a result of one's focus and commitment. The discouraging moments occur when one takes his/her eyes off of the finish line. One can easily adopt a secular perspective rather than a spiritual one in assessing one's success or failure; viability or necessity.

Most of us are familiar with the shelf-life of food items. When the expiration date approaches, items are usually discounted in the hope that the business loss will not be too great. Regrettably, shelf-life occurs in places other than a super-market or bakery where items that are no longer desirable are taken from the shelves and removed from circulation. This also happens with people. It can happen with one's job where layoffs occur to needed employees. However, the Church is also a place where shelf-life becomes a factor. Statistics show that ministers relocate to other pastoral locations within a five-year time frame. A church decides a minister is no longer necessary and a change needs to be made. The minister doesn't have much of a chance to change that thinking even though he is not in accord with that rationale. The Apostle Paul had a thought about such an event.

In First Corinthians 9:24-27, he references an athlete who strives for the award. He ends that illustration referencing his own discipline – "lest after preaching to others I myself should be disqualified."

In June 2020, Chuck Swindoll shared devotional thoughts about God's Waiting Room. He wrote:

> Some of you who read these words today could use a little extra hope, especially if you find yourself in a waiting mode. You were once engaged in the action, doing top-priority work on the front lines. No longer. All that has changed. Now, for some reason, you're on the shelf. It's tough to stay encouraged perched on a shelf. Your mind starts playing tricks on you. Though you are well-educated, experienced, and fairly gifted in your particular field, you are now waiting. You're wondering, and maybe you're getting worried, that this waiting period might be permanent. You can't see any light at the end of the tunnel. It just doesn't seem fair. After all, you've trained hard, you've jumped through hoops, and you've even made the necessary sacrifices. Discouragement crouches at the door, ready to pounce on any thought or hope, so you sit wondering why God has chosen to pass you by.

While this devotional addresses situations where one has been ministering, it can also be true in every day life. You have been well received in your job and gained promotions and positions. But suddenly, you've been let go and you wonder why. You begin to feel rejection and have a sense that you are no longer wanted or deemed to be necessary. Becoming expendable is a very difficult to swallow!

It is always encouraging and refreshing to read Isaiah 40:27-31. The Prophet Isaiah writes:

> Why do you say: My way is hidden from the LORD, and my right is disregarded by my God? Have you not known? Have you not heard? The LORD is the everlasting God, the Creator of the ends of the earth. He does not faint or grow weary; His understanding is unsearchable. He gives power to the faint, and to him who has no might He increases strength. Even youths shall faint and be weary, and young men shall fall exhausted; but they who wait for the LORD shall renew their strength; they shall mount up with wings like eagles; they shall run and not be weary; they shall walk and not faint.

Waiting for the Lord's timing and action is never easy. Most tend to be involved in doing, working, and planning. James Stalker wrote: "Waiting is a common instrument of providential discipline for those to whom exceptional work has been appointed." Waiting has occurred for hundreds who leave the ministry every year even while hundreds of churches are shuttered. Congregants and leaders continue with their age old philosophy of ministry despite the declines and possible ship-wrecks. They are more committed to traditions and buildings than they are to the welfare and spiritual growth of people.

In 1901, Irvin H. Mack wrote the words to a hymn entitled Light Beyond The Shadows. Some of the Lyrics are:

Though you cannot fathom
Why you're called to bear
All the heavy burdens That you cannot share,
Keep the cross before you In the darkest day;
Put your trust in Jesus All along the way.

Go with faith to conquer Trials that appear;
Know that Christ your Savior
With His help is near;
Never give up the battle,
Hard though it may be,
For your Lord has promised You -
The victory.

Where is one's safe place to be during relocations or being put on the shelf? While in God's Waiting Room, how should one respond or feel? My friend (Steve Sellers) clings to Psalm 91, especially the words in verses 1 and 2:

He who dwells in the shelter of the Most High will abide in the shadow of the Almighty. I will say to the LORD, You are my refuge and my fortress, my God, in whom I trust.

The shelter of the Lord is a great place to abide and to patiently wait. Does one know when, where, or how one will be moved from God's waiting room or removed from the shelf and found to be useful once again? No! That factor does not negate one's faith, trust and hope remaining in God alone.

God will (always) make a way
Where there seems to be no way!
He works in ways we cannot see –
He will make a way for me.
He WILL make a way!

As one pursues the mind and will of Jesus Christ, we must always be confident in the Him. He knows who and where we are! He knows the longing of one's heart and His plans for one's life. We should always remember Philippians 1:6 (NKJV), "Being confident of this very thing, that He who has begun a good work in you will complete it until the day of Jesus Christ..." Connected to this should also be Philippians 2:13, "It is God who works in you both to will and to do of His good pleasure."

Chapter Five - PERSPICACITY

Personal study of Scripture is very fulfilling. One method used to study the Bible is to note certain key phrases and pursue (cross-references) how they are used in other places of the Bible. As one reads and searches the Scriptures, perspicacity (a ready insight; shrewdness) can become a useful tool in one's understanding, decision-making and choices.

An example of phrase study would be a "Grasshopper Mentality." Numbers 13:33 mentions this when the spies returned from The Promised Land. Ten of them said they were positive about the abundance they observed as they travelled throughout the land. However, they were very apprehensive about the people who lived in that land. Their observation was: "We saw Giants there... Next to them we felt like grasshoppers, and that's what they thought, too!" Their negative perspective outweighed the positive and sufficiently caused the people to become faint-hearted and discouraged.

In Judges 7:11-12, grasshoppers once again became descriptive of the opposition that was awaiting the Israelites. Gideon and Purah, his servant, went down to the outposts of the camp. The Midianites, the Amalekites and all the other eastern peoples had settled in the valley, thick as locusts (grasshoppers). Their camels could no more be counted than the sand on the seashore. This was a factor in questioning how a few would be able to conquer the many. The multitude of "grasshoppers" was sufficient enough to cause Gideon and his servant to see how easily they could and would be facing an undefeatable multitude and an insurmountable population.

In a comparative way, we gain a glimpse of the perspicacity of the Eternal God as He views and acts on behalf of His creation. Isaiah 40:22 records God's view of His world: "God sits above the circle of the earth. The people below seem like grasshoppers to him!" At this writing, there are more than seven billion people throughout the world. I remember well when a visiting minister stated in his sermon that one would do well to think of himself/herself as being just one-seventh-billion in the global population. His message was addressing one's ego and sense of individual significance.

There are other beneficial studies in Scripture. One study is to locate the "Let Us" passages. This phrase is not a mere suggestion but a personal directive. A primary place to begin the study is Psalm 95:1-2,

> Come, LET US sing for joy to the Lord; LET US shout aloud to the Rock of our salvation. LET US come before him with thanksgiving and (LET US) extol him with music and song.

This phrase is scattered throughout the Psalms and elsewhere. Several "LET US" references can be located in the book of Hebrews, especially chapter 10.

Another important focus are the "One Another" passages in Scripture (especially in the New Testament). Some who have done linguistic research have determined there are 100 (more or less) "One Another/Each Other" references, especially in the New Testament. It must also be noted that 59 of these references are specific directives (commands) of what one is to become and be in terms of the practical applications stated.

One of the "One Another" references pertains to one's edification and application: To Love One Another. Jesus stated to His disciples after He had washed their feet (John 13:34-35):

> A new commandment I give to you, that you Love One Another just as I have loved you, you also are to Love One Another. By this all people will know that you are my disciples, if you have Love For One Another.

What is Jesus emphasizing with His disciples? Why is He repetitive in the emphasis? What is His expectation for all of His disciples in all generations? If He observed your life and mine, would He find us obedient to His directive?

First Corinthians 13 is a very practical mirror for the Biblical Christian to stand before and see the true reflection of what he or she is really like in His sight. What is the mirror-image in your mirror? As we consider this we should remember the words in James 1:22-24,

> Don't just listen to God's word. You must do what it says. Otherwise, you are only fooling yourselves. For if you listen to the word and don't obey, it is like glancing at your face in a mirror. You see yourself, walk away, and forget what you look like.

The Word of God emphasizes practical concerns for the Biblical Christian. As Jesus trained the twelve to be His disciples, those inspired to write the Scriptures also emphasized how the Biblical Christian is to live. It is vital that one develops a daily discipline of reading the Holy Scriptures for instruction, guidelines and preparation for serving the Lord Jesus Christ. In addition to the Holy Scriptures, familiarity with hymns also is of benefit. One hymn that could become a regular prayer of the child of God is:

Speak, Lord, in the stillness, While I wait on Thee; Hushed my heart to listen, In expectancy.

All to Thee is yielded, I am not my own; Blissful, glad surrender, I am Thine alone.

For the words Thou speakest, They are life indeed; Living bread from heaven, Now my spirit feed!

Fill me with the knowledge, Of Thy glorious will; All Thine own good pleasure In Thy child fulfill.

The goal for one's life is to be disciplined and consistent in pursuing the mind and will of Jesus Christ. In doing so, there will be a growing sense of living in the presence of God and knowing Him and His ways.

Chapter Six - CHOICE AND CHANGE

One of the primary functions in reading the Holy Scriptures is for the reader to gain a sense of God's thoughts, ways and mind. However, there are those who have read the Scriptures but decide to twist them to conform to their own personal bent. The Pharisees are an example. Jesus responded to them and others in accord with them,

> You do not have His word abiding in you, because whom He sent, Him you do not believe. You search the Scriptures, for in them you think you have eternal life; and these are they which testify of Me. But you are not willing to come to Me that you may have life." John 5:38-40 (NKJV).

Jesus also took the occasion to say in John 7:36, "Whoever believes in me, as the Scripture has said, Out of his heart will flow rivers of living water." The only way the Holy Scriptures can make a difference in one's life is through a personal relationship with Jesus Christ. With that relationship, there is also the assurance that the Holy Spirit will be available to guide one into a greater knowledge and application of God's Truth. Having shared the primary purpose of the Holy Spirit (John 16:7-11), Jesus goes on to assure His followers, "When He, the Spirit of truth, has come, He will guide you into all truth…He will tell you things to come. He will glorify Me…" John 16:13-14.

In 1982 Eddie Espinosa became a focal point because of his personal testimony and a prayer he wrote. The year was 1982. He wrote:

> I had been a Christian since 1969, but I saw a lot of things in my life that needed to be discarded. I had slowly become very complacent. I acknowledged my complacency, and I prayed to the Lord, The only way that I can follow you is for you to change my appetite, the things that draw me away. You must change my heart!
>
> Shortly thereafter I was in my car on the way to my work, feeling a desire to draw near to God and with the wrestling still going on in my heart.
>
> Suddenly, a melody and some words began to flood through my mind. As I stopped at a stop sign I reached for something to write on. The first thing I found was a small piece of yellow paper, which, by the way, I still have, and began to write as rapidly as I could. It was like taking dictation. I wrote the words on the paper, and kept the melody in my mind.

What was it that so captivated and impacted Eddie's heart and life? What were the words he wrote as they raced through his mind?

Change my heart, O God! Make it ever true.
Change my heart, O God! May I be like you.
You are the potter, I am the clay.
Mold me and make me, This is what I pray.

Eddie has had many great experiences with his chorus, Change My Heart, O God. He was privileged to lead thousands of men as they sang it at a Promise Keepers meeting at Texas Stadium in Dallas. The essence of Eddie's song is a prayer asking God to change us, making our hearts true, and changing us into the image of Jesus Christ.

Each one is confronted with the directives of Jesus Christ for anyone and all who would follow Him. First and foremost is to love the Lord with all of one's heart, Luke 10:27. The Psalmist clearly understood this necessity when he prayed in Psalm 139:23, "Search me, O God, and know my heart…"

A Hymn written by William C. Martin in the late 1800s is not well known nor is it often sung. The words are focused on the affections of one's heart and life.

I bring my heart to Thee,
My ills I cannot count,
That it may pure and cleansed be,
In Thy once opened fount.
Refrain:
I will no more delay,
Before Thy throne I fall,
And at Thy precious feet I lay
My heart, my life, my all.

On February 08, 2019 Charles Swindoll posted a devotional entitled: A Cheerful Heart.

Earthquakes! Prison riots! Economic pressures! Divorce! No jobs! Drugs! Disease! Death! Pretty serious scene, isn't it? Yet that is the emotional environment in which we live…

In spite of these bleak surroundings, or perhaps because of them, I firmly believe we need a good dose of Solomon's counsel. Listen to David's wisest son (Proverbs 13:15, 17:22):

A joyful heart makes a cheerful face, but when the heart is sad, the spirit is broken…All the days of the afflicted are bad, but a cheerful heart has a continual feast…A joyful heart is good medicine [the Hebrew says, 'causes good healing'], but a broken spirit dries up the bones…

Have you begun to shrivel into a bitter, impatient, critical Christian? The Lord tells us that the solution is simple: A joyful heart is what we need…and if ever we needed it, it is now.

James M. Gray and William Houghton were two great, godly men of the Word. Dr. Houghton writes of an occasion when he and Dr. Gray were praying together. Dr. Gray, though getting up in years, was still interested in being an effective witness and expositor. He concluded his prayer by saying: And, Lord, keep me cheerful. Keep me from becoming a cranky, old man!

If one is to ever know what it is to pursue the mind and will of Jesus Christ, it will include being like those attending Promise Keepers more than a generation ago. It necessitates one's echoing the words of impact and prayer:

Change MY heart, O God! Make it ever true.
Change MY heart, O God! May I be like you.

Let this be your/our choice. May we be focused and committed to being changed – more conformed to the image of the Lord Jesus Christ.

Chapter Seven - MORE THAN TOLERANCE

One of the intents of the "one another" directives in the Word of God is to the end that they affect and are incorporated into one's life. How one interacts with others discloses the degree to which the "one another" directives are believed and genuinely practiced. An extension of the "love one another" directives is amplified in Romans 12:10, "Love one another with brotherly affection and take delight in honoring each other" (that is, outdoing one another in showing honor).

The Amplified Bible states: "Be devoted to one another with [authentic] brotherly affection [as members of one family], give preference to one another in honor…" The ESV rendering is: "Love one another with brotherly affection. outdo one another in showing honor."

The idea is to convey an exuberance regarding one's affection and esteem toward all other brothers and sisters in Christ. It disallows the concept of "tolerating" another person even though one would rather not have to do so. The New Oxford American Dictionary defines honor as: "Holding one in high respect and great esteem; Something (or someone) regarded as a rare opportunity and privilege of bringing pride and pleasure to others."

The Bible uses the word honor. In Exodus 20:12, (the fifth commandment) God wanted His people to know, love and appreciate one's parents – "Honor your father and mother, so that you may live long in the land the Lord your God is giving you" This command is reiterated several times over again – (Matthew 9:19, Ephesians 6:1-3).

In general, how can one carefully display honor to another, especially if that person is not well known. If one is in a public setting and an unknown person is called upon to pray, is an immediate sense of caution present? An unidentified person wrote the following in September 2020. The author wrote:

A while back I read a story of a visiting pastor who attended a men's breakfast in the middle of a rural farming area of the country.

The group had asked an older farmer, decked out in bib overalls, to say grace for the morning breakfast.

The farmer began his prayer: "Lord, I hate buttermilk,"

The visiting pastor opened one eye to glance at the farmer and wondered where this was going.

The farmer then loudly proclaimed: "Lord, I hate lard."

Now the pastor was growing concerned.

Without missing a beat, the farmer continued: "And Lord, you know I don't much care for raw white flour."

The pastor once again opened an eye to glance around the room and saw that he wasn't the only one to feel uncomfortable.

Then the farmer added: "But Lord, when you mix them all together and bake them, I do love warm fresh biscuits."

So Lord, when things come up that we don't like, when life gets hard, when we don't understand what you're saying to us, help us to just relax and wait until you are done mixing. It will probably be even better than biscuits. Amen.

The person who posted the above went on to add:

Within that prayer there is great wisdom for all when it comes to complicated situations like we are experiencing in the world today. Stay strong, my friends, because our LORD is mixing several things that we don't really care for, but something even better is going to come when HE is done with it. Amen!

Amid the turmoil and uncertain times each one experiences, how does honor become a viable response? How can one honor the one who is in a position of authority but who represent godless and unrighteous principles? Can a child of God show honor and maintain inner perfect peace when anti-Christian positions are being espoused and effort is made to bring about compliance to the new directions?

In a world where turmoil occurs and disinformation is in the forefront, we have the words of Jesus Christ who told His disciples, (John 16:1, 33 NLT),

I have told you these things so that you won't abandon your faith... I have said these things to you, that in me you may have peace. In the world you will have tribulation. But take heart; I have overcome the world.

Are these words of Jesus Christ words that are willingly believed and embraced by the Biblical Christian? Do they inspire one to show respect for those in authority; to render to Caesar the things that are Caesar's; and to honor the king (First Peter 2:17)? In a day of persecution, note the terse and clear directives: "Honor everyone. Love the brotherhood. Fear God. Honor the emperor/king."

It reminds one of the hymn that challenges how one thinks and what one realizes about the lifestyle of God's people. The hymn asks and answers:

Peace, perfect peace, in this dark world of sin?
The blood of Jesus whispers peace within.

Peace, perfect peace, by thronging duties pressed?
To do the will of Jesus, this is rest.

Peace, perfect peace, death shadowing us and ours?
Jesus has vanquished death and all its powers.

Peace, perfect peace, our future all unknown?
Jesus we know, and he is on the throne.

(Then this glorious conclusion and assertion)
It is enough: earth's struggles soon shall cease,
And Jesus call us to heaven's perfect peace.

The pursuit of the mind and will of Jesus Christ will confront challenging times and people. Even though the challenge is real or severe, it must not deter one's focus on Jesus Christ. The goal and purpose is not prevented by the challenge but by one's surrender to circumstances. At a crucial moment during World War II, the Prime Minister, Winston Churchill, summoned the courage and confidence of the British people with a speech that included the following words:

> We shall go on to the end. We shall fight in France, we shall fight on the seas and oceans, we shall fight with growing confidence and growing strength in the air, we shall defend our island, whatever the cost may be. We shall fight on the beaches, we shall fight on the landing grounds, we shall fight in the fields and in the streets, we shall fight in the hills; we shall never surrender...

One's pursuit must have confidence and courage to be committed to knowing the mind and will of Jesus Christ. No circumstance or secular pressure should be allowed to dissuade one from the purpose to keep on looking to Jesus Christ   alone.

Chapter Eight - BE SILENT NO LONGER

In pursuing the thought, mind and will of Jesus Christ, is silence the direction that should be sought and practiced? A term used in the 1960s, The Silent Majority, was intended to describe a vast number of people in the nation. A summation statement expressed: "The silent majority is an unspecified large group of people in a country or group who do not express their opinions publicly." Even while the United States President, Richard M. Nixon, was attempting to rally the conservatives for a response to the Viet Nam War, he was assuming there was a "silent majority" who agreed with his assessments. Despite that assumption, however, the term did not emerge in public discourse until it was used by both Ronald Reagon and Donald Trump.

Today, in regard to beliefs and practices, does a large cross-section of the Biblical Church fall into the silent majority category? There are three references that should be considered.

First, we examine the confrontation between Israel and the Philistines (First Samuel 17). The champion of the Philistines was Goliath. He ridiculed and intimidated the Children of Israel and demeaned the name of God. King Saul and his army was well equipped but they cowered when Goliath bellowed out his demeaning words. They cringed in fear. First Samuel 17:11 indicates: "When Saul and all Israel heard these words of the Philistine, they were dismayed and greatly afraid."

When David came on the scene, he exuded his confidence and employed his skills to take on the giant. One thing is certain, David was not silent. When Goliath appeared and voiced his disdain of the boy David, David ran toward him and said (First Samuel 17:45-46):

> You come to me with a sword and with a spear and with a javelin, but I come to you in the name of the LORD of hosts, the God of the armies of Israel, whom you have defied. This day the LORD will deliver you into my hand, and I will strike you down and cut off your head.

David's words were not boasting nor was he intimidated by the adversary. They were accurately stated and he accomplished what he set out to do.

A second reference about a silent majority is found in First Kings 18 when the prophet of God, Elijah, addressed King Ahab and the people. The issue was the dominance of the prophets of Baal and the acts of Jezebel against the prophets of God. At a particular point, Elijah challenged the people (First Kings 18:21), "How long will you go limping between two different opinions? If the LORD is God, follow him; but if Baal, then follow him." A clear choice amid a dominant reign of a King and his ambitious and godless wife, Jezebel. How will the people respond in the presence of the Prophet, but much more importantly, in the presence of The

Lord? While one would hope for a positive and encouraging response, how did the people respond? The people preferred silence rather that asserting any confidence in the Lord. The descriptive words were: "And the people did not answer him a word." After the display of God's power, the people responded (Verse 39): "And when all the people saw it, they fell on their faces and said, "The LORD, he is God; the LORD, He is God."

Is this the method for one's pursuit of the thought, mind and will of Jesus Christ? Is one called to be a part of the Silent Majority? Is it a posture that brings glory and honor to Jesus Christ? Does it result in the Lord withholding His power in the "professing Christian"?

A third reference is when Jesus Christ enunciates the rightful place for His followers to speak up and stand up! In John 12:13 we read about the triumphal entry into Jerusalem: "When Jesus rode into Jerusalem on a colt of a donkey, the people shouted, Hosanna! Blessed is he who comes in the name of the Lord, even the King of Israel." This was met with the negative words (Luke 19:39), "Some of the Pharisees in the crowd said to him: Teacher, rebuke your disciples." The desire of the Pharisees to have a silent majority is addressed by Jesus Christ (Luke 19:40), "I tell you, if these (crowds of people) were silent, the very stones would cry out." The force of not being silent was summed up in a worship chorus:

All hail King Jesus, All hail Emmanuel;
King of Kings, Lord of Lords -
Bright Morning Star.

And throughout eternity, I'll sing Your praises;
And I'll reign with You throughout eternity!

There are times and situations when the Lord uses what He has created to indicate His presence. One such moment occurs after Elijah's great sense of God's power in confronting the prophets of Baal. But then, we find that Elijah flees when he hears the threats of Jezebel against him (First Kings 19). Can Elijah escape from the presence of Jezebel? Yes! Can he escape from the presence of God? No! Elijah hides in the shelter of a cave. He feels safe there. But then, God comes and speaks to him first through the elements and then with His actual words "in a low whisper." The summary is found in First Kings 19:11-12. God said:

> Go out and stand on the mount before the LORD. And behold, the LORD passed by, and a great and strong wind tore the mountains and broke in pieces the rocks before the LORD, but the LORD was not in the wind. And after the wind an earthquake, but the LORD was not in the earthquake. And after the earthquake a fire, but the LORD was not in the fire. And after the fire the sound of a low whisper (a still small voice.

It is a fallacy to think that one can escape God and His requirements. He wants His people to know and have the thoughts, mind and will of Jesus Christ. One may run and try to hide. But no one can escape the presence of God. The Lord may be ready to speak to you "in a low whisper" (a still small voice) so you will get back on track and declare His gospel and glory. Are you listening?

Chapter Nine - HOPE FOR THE HOPELESS

A focus one should always retain is to look first to Jesus and avoid looking at one's circumstances unless or until done by looking to Jesus Christ alone (Hebrews 12:2). It is also good to remember the concluding words of First Corinthians 13. It is a chapter that usually brings to mind the emphasis on what love is and means. However, First Corinthians 13:13 states: "Three things will last forever; faith, hope, and love…" These principles are meshed together for every child of God.

The words written about Abraham should be encouraging for all followers of Jesus Christ. Romans 4:18-21 shares with us the hope that Abraham never relinquished:

> Even when there was no reason for hope, Abraham kept hoping and believing that he would become the father of many nations. For God had said to him, That's how many descendants you will have! And Abraham's faith did not weaken, even though, at about 100 years of age, he figured his body was as good as dead as was Sarah's womb. Abraham never wavered in believing God's promise. In fact, his faith grew stronger, and in this he brought glory to God. He was fully convinced that God is able to do whatever he promises.

In Genesis 12, God had promised Abraham that he would be the father of many nations. His family would be greater than the stars in heaven or the grains of sand. Would this happen immediately? No! Abraham had no idea when it would transpire or how great in number his heirs would be. As Paul reminded us, Abraham received a promise from God and never wavered in his faith and never surrendered his hope. He understood God had a perfect plan and all he needed to do was to fit his life into that plan.

To the persecuted believers in Thessalonica, Paul wrote words of encouragement and hope,

> Dear brothers and sisters, we can't help but thank God for you, because your faith is flourishing and your love for one another is growing. We proudly tell God's other churches about your endurance and faithfulness in all the persecutions and hardships you are suffering. And God will use this persecution to show his justice and to make you worthy of his Kingdom, for which you are suffering (Second Thessalonians 1:3-5).

Peter was also writing to a persecuted Church. He began his words of encouragement and instruction with:

> Blessed be the God and Father of our Lord Jesus Christ! According to his great mercy, he has caused us to be born again to a living hope through the resurrection of Jesus Christ from the dead (First Peter 1:3, ESV).

To those who knew affliction and death could be imminent, Peter reminded them of the "living hope" that was theirs because of the resurrection of Jesus Christ. Peter reminds the people they are to be strong in their faith. In Second Peter 3:13 (ESV), the people are reminded about the promises of God: "But according to His promise we are waiting for new heavens and a new earth in which righteousness dwells." In this text, Peter is linking faith, endurance and expectation (hope) as interdependent upon each other.

In one's pursuit of the Lord's thoughts, mind and will, one will have to be prepared for a long journey and walk. God's timetable does not conform to one's desires or circumstances. We may long for His return and our being caught up to be with Him. That will require patient endurance. In His time, one's trials will be ended and the burdens of life lifted. Some words of hope one should embrace are:

Matthew 11:28-30, Jesus said:

> Come to me, all of you who are weary and carry heavy burdens, and I will give you rest. Take my yoke upon you. Let me teach you, because I am humble and gentle at heart, and you will find rest for your souls. For my yoke is easy to bear, and the burden I give you is light.

Isaiah 40:1-2 (NLT - Personalized)

Comfort, comfort my people, says your God. Speak tenderly…Tell them that their sad days are gone and her sins are pardoned.

Hymns are also beneficial for one's encouragement and hope, especially during times of adversity.

My hope is built on nothing less
Than Jesus' blood and righteousness…
His oath, His covenant, His blood,
Support me in the whelming flood.
When all around my soul gives way,
He then is all my hope and stay.

On Christ, the solid Rock I stand.
All other ground is sinking sand.

An additional hymn that reminds one of the completed work of Jesus Christ is:

My Hope is in the Lord, who gave Himself for me
And paid the price of all my sin at Calvary.

No merit of my own His anger to suppress,
My only hope is found in Jesus' righteousness.
Refrain:
For me He died; For me He lives,
And everlasting life and light He freely gives.

Child of God, as you pursue the mind and will of Jesus Christ, keep looking to Him at all times and for all things. Don't let your changing circumstances crush your spirit or diminish your hope in the Lord. You are held secure in the hand of God the Father and God the Son (John 10:28-30). He will keep and preserve you. You are precious to Him and He'll never forget you or let go of you. The affirmation of The Good Shepherd who calls His sheep by name knows your name. His spoken words are for your encouragement and perseverance. Jesus will never fail you! He wants you to be guarded that you don't fail Him.

Chapter Ten - COMFORT AVAILABILITY

A previous chapter offered the words of the prophet Isaiah where the Lord wants His people to be reminded of His mind and will: "Comfort, comfort my people, says your God. Speak tenderly…"(Isaiah 40:1). There is a role for God's people to offer comfort to those who have experienced hardship, sorrow, disaster and difficulties almost beyond description. What words should be foremost in the minds and heart of God's people? First Corinthians 1:3-5 (ESV) recognizes the source and instructs the practical use of the comfort that is available:

> Blessed be the God and Father of our Lord Jesus Christ, the Father of mercies and God of all comfort, who comforts us in all our affliction, so that we may be able to comfort those who are in any affliction, with the comfort with which we ourselves are comforted by God. For as we share abundantly in Christ's sufferings, so through Christ we share abundantly in comfort too.

There are many illustrations where Jesus Christ is the example and advocate of comfort. During a ferocious storm that threaten lives (Mark 4), Jesus calmly says to the frightened disciples and tempestuous sea: "Peace! Be still!" To the anxious and sorrowing sisters and friends of Lazarus who has died (John 11), Jesus said: "I AM the resurrection and the life. Do you believe this?" He then calls Lazarus to exit his burial place. When He advises the disciples that he will not remain with them and observes their troubled hearts and minds (John 16:16-24), Jesus said: "I say to you, you will weep and lament, but the world will rejoice. You will be sorrowful, but your sorrow will turn into joy." What did Jesus mean and intend with His statement? He had already expressed to them (John 16:5-15 KJV),

> I tell you the truth; It is expedient for you that I go away: for if I go not away, the Comforter (Helper, Advocate) will not come unto you; but if I depart, I will send him unto you.

In 1890, Frank Bottome wrote words that were in his mind and heart:

> O spread the tidings 'round,
> Wherever man is found,
> Wherever human hearts
> And human woes abound;
> Let every Christian tongue
> Proclaim the joyful sound:
> The Comforter has come!

In 1876, after Horatio G. Spafford heard of his four daughters being drowned at sea, in this moment of tragedy, grief and sorrow, he penned the well-known words that were in his mind and heart, words that brought him comfort in the midst of personal adversity:

> When peace, like a river,

Attendeth my way,
When sorrows like sea billows roll;
Whatever my lot,
Thou has taught me to say,
It is well, it is well, with my soul.

Despite the storm that had drowned his daughters, despite the inner turmoil of his personal grief and sorrow, he had comfort in his spirit, mind and heart that circumstances did not govern his life. He already had come to a settled commitment in his relationship to Jesus Christ. This event would not dissuade him from his journey with the Lord.

In 1563, there was a Creedal Statement formulated at the request of Elector Frederick III who ruled the province of the Palatinate from 1559 to 1576. He encouraged a system of Biblical instruction for the people under his authority. Later, in 1619, the Synod of Dordt approved the words published in the Heidelberg Catechism for use and instruction in the churches. It begins with this question and answer:

Question 1:

What is your only comfort in life and in death?

Answer 1:

That I am not my own, but belong in body and soul, in life and in death to my faithful Savior, Jesus Christ. He has fully paid for all my sins with his precious blood, and has set me free from the tyranny of the devil. He also watches over me in such a way that not a hair can fall from my head without the will of my Father in heaven; in fact, all things must work together for my salvation. Because I belong to him, Christ, by his Holy Spirit, assures me of eternal life[9] and makes me wholeheartedly willing and ready from now on to live for him.

It would serve all of us well if we recalled the words to a traditional Christmas carol, God Rest Ye Merry Gentlemen. Some of the lyric that should not go unnoticed are:

Let nothing you dismay,
Remember Christ our Savior
was born on Christmas Day;
To save us all from Satan's power
when we were gone astray.
O tidings of comfort and joy…

The phrase "comfort and joy" are repeated three times in the refrain. Are these the words – "Comfort and Joy"-resonating within you? What is YOUR only comfort in life and in death? Does it begin with: "I am not my own, but belong in body and soul, in life and in death to my faithful Savior, Jesus Christ"? You can and should have comfort and peace from the Lord whom you love and live for. A song of your mind and heart could be – should be:

Like a river glorious
Is God's perfect peace,
Over all victorious
In its bright increase;

Perfect, yet it floweth Fuller every day,
Perfect, yet it growth
Deeper all the way.
Refrain:
Stayed upon Jehovah,
Hearts are fully blest;
Finding, as He promised,
Perfect peace and rest.

May you know the reality a cannot give. So don't be troubled or afraid" (John 14:27, NLT).

Chapter Eleven - CARING

For many years, the Hallmark Greeting Card Company had as a slogan: "When you care enough to send the very best." The company focus was to create cards that were unique and would give the recipient a sense that they were cared for in a special way. Hallmark's success depended on that result for their product – a greeting card. When it comes to people, especially for those who are committed within a Biblical Church, is there a sense that as individuals we care enough to give the Lord our very best?

There is an abbreviated statement that speaks volumes. It is: "Who cares?" It can be an expression of indifference or it can express despair and hopelessness. It can even be a negative commentary on a sermon that has just been preached. As people leave the church service, they can express at least one of two critiques: "Who really cares?" or "So what?" Either expression has a similar meaning of a remaining emptiness that has not been met by interaction with a "professing Christian" or by a casual, lackadaisical sermon presentation. A sermon containing words that were absent of practical application for them.

In a personal and practical way, what should true Biblical caring look like? By what standard could that be measured? When individuals are pursuing the mind and will of Jesus Christ, what does caring truly mean? How observable will that be?

An inappropriate response is stated in James 2:2-3 (NLT):

> For example, suppose someone comes into your meeting dressed in fancy clothes and expensive jewelry, and another comes in who is poor and dressed in dirty clothes. If you give special attention and a good seat to the rich person, but you say to the poor one: You can stand over there, or else sit on the floor - well, doesn't this discrimination show that your judgments are guided by evil motives?

As unacceptable as this approach is, James goes deeper into the caring-factor as he personalizes one's response to human need and one's caring response.

> What good is it, dear brothers and sisters, if you say you have faith but don't show it by your actions? Can that kind of faith save anyone? Suppose you see a brother or sister who has no food or clothing, and you say: Good-bye and have a good day; stay warm and eat well - but then you don't give that person any food or clothing. What good does that do? James 2:13-16 (NLT).

One's response would want to express: "I would never knowingly let that happen!" Really? There are people who carry burdens who feel all alone as they struggle along in life. Recently, I was in Walmart looking for an item. A woman was on the same aisle and wanted a heavier item on an upper shelf that was not within her reach. I offered to help her and she was appreciative. In the process, I mentioned a statement I had made to one of my daughters. I asked this woman: "Have you ever bet someone that you could not find an item they were sure would be on the shelf." It was a rhetorical question. However, the woman began to pour out her heart and mind about a 37 year old daughter who was addicted to drugs and mood modifiers. This heart-broken mother shared how she had tried everything with no positive result. After several minutes of listening, and as she paused to see if I had really been listening, I shared with her how my wife and I were very concerned for someone we knew who had made some very negative choices in life. I asked the woman I was visiting with: "Have you ever raised your uplifted hands to the Lord and said: "Lord, I have done all I know to do in this person's behalf! I am giving her into your hands! I let go! Please work in this person's life." Her response was not in terms of faith and prayer. She indicated that she had knocked her down on the floor, sat on top of her and wagged her finger at her. Shocking response and behavior? Yes!

I tried to remind her that tough love did not include that type of physical response. This addicted person was her daughter and as her mother she may be the last best chance for her daughter changing her lifestyle choices. The woman looked at me, hesitatingly and then, went on her way. This generated a question within me in two ways: (1) How many people cross our paths and have similar cares and needs? (2) Have you/I started a conversation with a stranger to pass the time of day or to ask how they are getting along? In doing so, one will never know what cares are becoming a burden in one's life. Yesterday, I spoke with a woman who was looking at various items on the day-old bakery rack. I mentioned there were many fine looking and tempting items. At this point, she indicated she should not be doing that because she had become a diabetic. Did I know this woman? No! I had never seen her before. She seemed eager to speak with someone about her physical concern.

I often feel conviction when reading the Olivet Discourse, especially Matthew 25 where Jesus is separating the sheep from the goats. In verses 31-46, Jesus Christ wants to determine whether or not one has expressed genuine and deliberate care for others with practical needs. In Matthew 25:35-36 (NLT), Jesus stated to the sheep:

> I was hungry, and you fed me. I was thirsty, and you gave me a drink. I was a stranger, and you invited me into your home. I was naked, and you gave me clothing. I was sick, and you cared for me. I was in prison, and you visited me.

When the sheep interacted with others, was it a forced act on their part? No! It was a response based upon the sheep who had heard their shepherd's voice and followed Him.

Those categorized as "goats" indicated they were unaware of the needs Jesus was mentioning! Their question to Jesus was: When did we see you in need? Jesus' answer is simply and plainly: If you did it in behalf of one of the least of these with cares, needs and burdens, you did it unto Me. The guideline is: Be Aware So You Can/Will Care! Are you one of the Shepherd's sheep? You can be! Listen to His voice and follow Him! Care enough to do your very best in the name of your Savior and Shepherd!

Chapter Twelve - A PURPOSE FOR LIVING

Have you ever given any thought about your life and your purpose for living? There is a place in one's life for the creedal statement that asks and answers: What is the chief end of man? Man's chief end is to glorify God and enjoy Him forever. If glorifying God is the chief end, how can one apply that truth during a time of uncertainty and/or medical unknowns? When there is a pondering of life and death issues, how should one respond and react?

The whole idea of living caused me to be startled by a question when I went for my first treatment of chemotherapy. Before the treatment was started, there was a brief interview. The first question asked was: "In the past two weeks, have you ever considered ending your life?" I was surprised by the question but it caused me to be reflective about my purpose for living. I had always glibly indicated that pursuing the mind and will of Jesus Christ was primary. But – was it? When facing the potential of dying, does a purpose for living control one's thoughts and mindsets? I returned home and worked diligently on business matters that would make it easier for my wife if I was no longer alive. Sobering? Yes! Emotional? Yes!

After the third or fourth interview when the same question was asked, I posed a question. Do you really expect a person to honestly answer your question? The interviewer quickly answered: "Yes! As a matter of fact, we have had several patients who saw ending their own life as the best option rather than the extensive treatment regimen." Later on, in an infusion area next to mine, I heard the Doctor indicate to his patient that he had exhausted all of the treatments he knew of and that the man may have only three weeks remaining to live. I overheard the man and his son beg the Doctor to try other treatments. The Doctor indicated that he had done all that he could do.

When my treatment for the day concluded, the son was sitting in the reception area with a very sad and dejected expression. I tried to speak with him about the news they had received. His response was mindboggling when he said: "We go to a Baptist Church and we'll be alright." Being in a church does not make one a child of God anymore than being in a garage would make one a car. Church membership is fine but is never a substitute for one's personal relationship to and trust in Jesus Christ.

Additionally, to compound my thoughts about ending one's life, there was a series of suicides that came to my attention. Three of the people I had known. The fourth had been a minister who counselled troubled people about their lives and the meaning that was attached to them. Surprisingly, without any clear reason, he ended his own life and thus negatively impacting the lives of his wife and young children. The four suicides that occurred in fairly quick succession drove me to think further on the purpose for living pursuing the mind and will of Jesus Christ.

Gloria Gaither wrote lyrics for the tune Finlandia. Other hymns written to that tune are the familiar, "Be Still My Soul, The Lord is On Thy Side" and another lyric less known is: "We Rest On Thee, Our Shield and Our Defender." The lyric by Gloria Gaither is based upon the writing of Francis Schaeffer, How Then Shall We Live? The first few lines she wrote were of encouragement to me: "I then shall live as one who's been forgiven. I'll walk with joy to know my debts are paid. I know my name is clear before my Father; I am His child and I am not afraid." The words that resonate when one is pursuing the mind and will of Jesus Christ are: "I am His child and I am not afraid."

How did the Psalmist face his concerns? How did he deal with his threshold depression? Asaph had a great perspective when he penned Psalm 73:17-27. Regardless of the circumstances that could beleaguer one, he knew in his heart of hearts:

> I still belong to you; You hold my right hand. You guide me with your counsel, leading me to a glorious destiny. Whom have I in heaven but You? I desire You more than anything on earth. My health may fail, and my spirit may grow weak, but God remains the strength of my heart; He is mine forever…But as for me, how good it is to be near God! I have made the Sovereign LORD my shelter, and I will tell everyone about the wonderful things You do.

Vincent van Gogh (1853-1890), an impressionist artist in his short life, had produced more than 2100 paintings. However, he was not commercially successful and he ended his life at age 37. This came after years of mental illness, depression and poverty.

A song written about Vincent van Gogh was sung by Don McLane, "Starry, Starry Night." It is a haunting melody about a life that was unable to be fulfilled by the artist's gift ultimately reaching a point of ending where he ended his life. Ending one's life is a very sad decision and choice. It would be much better in moments of futility, stress and depression if one would give consideration to the prayer of Epaphras in Colossians 4:12, "He always prays earnestly for you, asking God to make you strong and perfect, fully confident that you are following the whole will of God." The Message paraphrase is: "Epaphras has been tireless in his prayers for you, praying that you'll stand firm, mature and confident in everything God wants you to do." It focuses one upon the importance of pursuing the mind and will of God in one's life.

How should one approach life in the 21st century? In 1824, William F. Lloyd wrote words that apply today:

My times are in Thy hand;
Whatever they may be;
Pleasing or painful, dark or bright,
As best may seem to Thee.

My times are in Thy hand,

I'll always trust in Thee;
And, after death, at Thy right hand
I shall forever be.

Chapter Thirteen - WORSHIP

Psalm 95:8-9 (NLT) is a basic guideline for one's worship of God:

> Oh come, let us worship and bow down; let us kneel before the LORD, our Maker! For he is our God, and we are the people of his pasture, and the sheep of his hand.

These verses indicate the act and posture that can be included as one worships the holy and living God. Jesus Christ gives a definition of worship in John 4:23-24 (ESV),

> The hour is coming, and is now here, when the true worshipers will worship the Father in spirit and truth, for the Father is seeking such people to worship him. God is spirit, and those who worship him must worship in spirit and truth.

A primary focus for worship is to have one's mind and will set on things above (Colossians 3:1-2). Also, it is valuing relationship and identity with the Sovereign God. It is an eagerness to respond positively to who He is and what He desires to receive from those who belong to Him. Some hymn writers and translators tried to define and give expression of true worship through their work. A hymn such as: "All Glory, Laud and Honor, To Thee Redeemer King" is one example.

David had a unique understanding of what true worship should include. When he penned Psalm 29, he began (Verses 1-2) with the words that elevated and enlarged his sense of the majesty and glory of the Lord:

> Ascribe to the LORD, O heavenly beings, Ascribe to
> the LORD glory and strength. Ascribe to
> the LORD the glory due his name; worship
> the LORD in the splendor of holiness.

The word ascribe means: "A quality that is due and belongs to another." In this usage by David, his approach was that all I can offer in the presence of God would still be inadequate when thought of in terms of the blessings and authority flowing from God to His creation. The sense of this is seen in the prayer offered by David in First Chronicles 29:10-12,

> Then David praised the LORD in the presence of the whole assembly: O LORD, the God of our ancestor Israel, may you be praised forever and ever! Yours, O LORD, is the greatness, the power, the glory, the victory, and the majesty. Everything in the heavens and on earth is yours, O LORD, and this is your kingdom. We adore you as the one who is over all things. Wealth and honor come from you alone, for you rule over everything. Power and might are in your hand, and at your discretion people are made great and given strength.

David's sense of worship may have influenced Isaiah to have a similar unique approach in his worship. Isaiah 6 finds the prophet, by means of a vision, in the very presence of God. He hears and sees angel choirs singing Holy, Holy, Holy. He sees the radiance of God's presence. As his vision continues, Isaiah realizes his personal need for confession (verse 5): "It's all over! I am doomed, for I am a sinful man. I have filthy lips, and I live among a people with filthy lips. Yet I have seen the King, the LORD…"

Both David and Isaiah influence one to have a more reverent approach in worship. A serious worship challenge is expressed in the words written by George Atlins (1819): "Brethren, we have met to worship and adore the Lord our God…Let us love our God supremely…" We may unite in singing or listening to the correct hymns, but do we have the awareness that true worship necessitates one's being in the presence of a Holy God who is to be worshipped in the beauty of His holiness?

In 1863, Joachim Neander was led to write about and express one's approach in worship: "Praise to the Lord, O let all that is in me adore Him! All that hath life and breath, Come now with praises before Him…"

One should often think of the importance of being in the presence of God. Based upon Psalm 16:11, Dick Tinney wrote the refrain:

In Your presence, there is comfort.
In Your presence, there is peace.

When we seek to know Your heart,
We will find such blessed assurance -
In Your holy presence Lord.

Revelation 22:3-5 provides clarity of one aspect of being in God's presence:

> No longer will there be anything accursed, but the throne of God and of the Lamb will be in it, and his servants will worship him. They will see his face, and his name will be on their foreheads. And night will be no more. They will need no light of lamp or sun, for the Lord God will be their light, and they will reign forever and ever.

John was excited and enthusiastic as he heard the words of the angel. He writes in Revelation 22:8-9,

> I, John, am the one who heard and saw these things. And when I heard and saw them, I fell down to worship at the feet of the angel who showed them to me, but he said to me: You must not do that! I am a fellow servant with you and your brothers the prophets, and with those who keep the words of this book. Worship God.

There is considerable variation in the way churches conduct worship services. Some are based upon traditions that have been established over the years. Others are committed to liturgy, form and ritual. Some modern approaches are casual and more entertaining than traditional. There is the thought that one can achieve balance to appeal to the greater numbers of people. Worship can sometimes become confused when the service is designed to appeal to people's wants rather than training people the reverence God seeks for Himself. Some gatherings of people (the church) need to learn more about what God wants rather than what they deem as appropriate.

At the very least, each day, may you radiate the beauty of holiness from being in the holy presence of the Lord and learning how to ascribe to the Lord the glory that is due to Him and His name. James Montgomery wrote the words in his Christmas Carol, Angels from The Realms of Glory, the grandiose opportunity for God's people to join with the Angel Choir who bids us to:

Come and worship, come and worship,
Worship Christ, the newborn King.

Chapter Fourteen - SUFFERING SERVANTS

If the average person was asked about suffering and what it represents, how do you think they would respond? Would they have a mental list of their personal ailments and limitations – arthritis; dental issues; handicaps of one sort or another; unaffordable medical care? Would they describe the various medications they are taking?

How many would share about scars from sharing Jesus Christ with a lost world? How many would recognize God's promises but acknowledge they haven't born fruition in their personal needs? How many would project beyond themselves and show meaningful concern for a family member, friend or a person of need (other than themselves)? Would there be any mention of those who are being persecuted because of their faith in Jesus Christ or because of their making Him known to others?

There are places in Scripture where suffering is described and how different ones have responded to that adversity. Some are mentioned in a chapter entitled Destined for Glory from the book Holiness Day By Day by Jerry Bridges:

> Paul wrote that our sufferings produce perseverance, which in turn produces character (Romans 5:3-4), and James said that the testing of our faith develops perseverance, which leads to maturity (James 1:2-5).

Our ultimate hope, though, is not in maturity of character in this life, as valuable as that is, but in the perfection of character in eternity. John wrote: When he appears, we shall be like him, for we shall see him as he is (1 John 3:2, NIV). The often painful process of being transformed into his likeness will be over. We shall be completely conformed to the likeness of the Lord Jesus Christ.

Paul wrote: I consider that our present sufferings are not worth comparing with the glory that will be revealed in us (Romans 8:18, NIV). I visualize in my mind a pair of old-fashioned balance scales. Paul first puts all our sufferings, heartaches, disappointments - all our adversities of whatever kind from whatever source - onto one side of the balance scales. Then he puts on the other side the glory that will be revealed in us. As we watch, the scales do not balance, but completely bottom out on the side of the glory that will be revealed in us.

There is a passage in Hebrews 11:32-38 (NLT) that is descriptive of the price that is often paid for one's stand for the Lord:

It would take too long to recount the stories of the faith of Gideon, Barak, Samson, Jephthah, David, Samuel, and all the prophets. By faith these people overthrew kingdoms, ruled with justice, and received what God had promised them. They shut the mouths of lions, quenched the flames of fire, and escaped death by the edge of the sword. Their weakness was turned to strength. They became strong in battle and put whole armies to flight…others were tortured, refusing to turn from God in order to be set free… Some were jeered at, and their backs were cut open with whips. Others were chained in prisons. some died by stoning, some were sawed in half, and others were killed with the sword. Some went about wearing skins of sheep and goats, destitute and oppressed and mistreated. They were too good for this world, wandering over deserts and mountains, hiding in caves and holes in the ground.

Paul sometimes mentioned his personal sufferings but despite them he persevered to carry out his assigned task. On a couple of occasions, he mentioned his hardships to make a point of the needed commitment to Jesus Christ. It was also his way of dealing with criticism that was directed at him. Second Corinthians 4:8-12 (NLT) expresses the commitment and purpose for his ongoing effort despite the prevailing dangers,

> We are pressed on every side by troubles, but we are not crushed. We are perplexed, but not driven to despair. We are hunted down, but never abandoned by God. We get knocked down, but we are not destroyed. Through suffering, our bodies continue to share in the death of Jesus so that the life of Jesus may also be seen

in our bodies. Yes, we live under constant danger of death because we serve Jesus, so that the life of Jesus will be evident in our dying bodies. So we live in the face of death, but this has resulted in eternal life for you.

Paul is bold to assert the favor of the Lord, Romans 8:17 (NLT):

Since we are his children, we are his heirs. In fact, together with Christ we are heirs of God's glory. But if we are to share his glory, we must also share his suffering.

A hymn written by Isaac Watts (1721)expresses the sentiments of Paul about being a suffering servant,

Am I a soldier of the cross,
A follower of the Lamb,
And shall I fear to own His cause,
Or blush to speak His name?

Must I be carried to the skies
On flowery beds of ease,
While others fought to win the prize,
And sailed through bloody seas?

Are there no foes for me to face?...

Sure I must fight if I would reign;
Increase my courage, Lord.
I'll bear the toil, endure the pain,
Supported by Thy Word.

May these words represent our commitment and readiness to be a suffering servant for Christ and His Kingdom. This is part of one's pursuit to gain insight into the Lord's thoughts, mind and will for His followers. It's not an easy commitment when deciding to be like Jesus. He stated as clearly as possible what it would mean for them to be identified with Him:

> If the world hates you, remember that it hated me first. The world would love you as one of its own if you belonged to it, but you are no longer part of the world. I chose you to come out of the world, so it hates you. Do you remember what I told you? A slave is not greater than the master. Since they persecuted me, naturally they will persecute you (John 15:18-20, NLT).

Chapter Fifteen - TIME-LINES

One of the more difficult learning experiences is to know how to wait patiently. Instant gratification seems to be ingrained within one from birth and throughout life. Some children (and people) exhibit, "I want what I want when I want it!" Where do you suppose they have learned that mindset? Is the skill of waiting patiently relevant for the professing Christian? Is it present within the culture where one lives?

We have heard and tritely used a hackneyed military expression where one is expected to "hurry up and wait." Waiting in any situation or context is not easy for most people. In fact, it could be a pet-peeve for all too many. Admittedly, it is frustrating to have an appointment set at a doctor's office (or elsewhere) where it has become a routine that the appointment time is constructed to have one in the waiting room for a set time before seeing the doctor. It may be for one-half hour, sometimes longer. And then, one's name is called and after triage, one is taken to an examining room and one spends more time waiting before the Doctor makes an appearance and asks: "How are you doing"? Most would rather avoid the frustration of the long wait and just want to get the examination so one can leave. It almost appears that the doctor is either oblivious or chooses to ignore the inordinate delay.

When it comes to the Biblical Christian's life and pursuing the mind and the will of God, the waiting time can cover a period of days, weeks, months or years. The child of God should be encouraged by knowing (and believing) words such as Jeremiah 29:11, "The Lord knows the plans that He has for us." Additionally, knowing and believing the words in Ephesians 1:4, "He chose us in him before the creation of the world to be holy and blameless in his sight…" We tend to treat these words in a generalized way rather than as stipulated facts and realities.

There are many lessons that can be learned from reviewing the life of the Psalmist. One of those lessons is in Psalm 37:7 (NIV), "Be still before the Lord and wait patiently for him…" The Message shares: "Quiet down before God, be prayerful before him. Don't bother with those who climb the ladder, who elbow their way to the top." The NKJV translation – "Rest (Relax) in the Lord, and wait patiently for Him…" One of the lessons the Psalmist incorporated into his life was developing the discipline to "wait patiently" for the Lord's guidance and will to be revealed. Is this easy to do? No! Do we need to develop this discipline? Yes! Psalm 46:10 (ESV) shares another aspect of waiting. It is to reflect and meditate on learning: "Be still, and know that I am God."

In 1824, William F. Lloyd wrote helpful words in a hymn that share the perspective of the Psalmists as they shared the lessons to be learned about waiting patiently:

My times are in Thy hand;
My God, I wish them there;

My life, my friends, my soul I leave
Entirely to Thy care.

My times are in Thy hand;
Whatever they may be;
Pleasing or painful, dark or bright,
As best may seem to Thee.

My times are in Thy hand;
Why should I doubt or fear?
My Father's hand will never cause
His child a needless tear.

The Lord often uses world events to gain the attention He deserves from His people. Time after time, the Lord used human resources and nations to bring His people to their senses and renew their dependence upon Him. Examples would be the various captivities His people had to endure due to their complacency and/or the hardness of their hearts. The children of Israel were in Egypt 400 years until Moses, at 80 years of age led God's people toward The Promised Land. As we move along in Biblical History, we arrive at the Babylonian Captivity and the disclosures in the Book of Daniel. After a lifetime in captivity, Daniel was the only one with the sense that the 70 years spoken of by Jeremiah was now nearing a conclusion.

Could it be that we are seeing the same type of events unfolding in our day? Is it possible that fires, hurricanes, earthquakes, plagues (pandemics), etc. are the means the Lord employs to get His people to seek Him and His will? Does He want His people to develop the discipline to wait patiently and to pursue His mind and will? Your answer to these questions should be: Yes! What hinders one from learning to wait? A simple answer is: impatience and wanting the result we want when we want it. How does Jesus Christ want His followers to respond to His readiness to share with them His mind and will? His answer was clearly stated in Matthew 11:28-30, "Come to Me…I will give you rest; Learn from Me…you will find rest for your soul…" What hinders one from responding to the invitation of Jesus Christ? Is He the authority in one's life or is "self" reluctant to relinquish that control to Him? The prayer of your heart and life can be (should be) the words written by Frances R. Havergal in 1874:

> Take my life, and let it be
> Consecrated, Lord, to Thee.
> Take my moments and my days…
>
> Take my will, and make it Thine;
> It shall be no longer mine.
> Take my heart, it is Thine own;
> It shall be Thy royal throne….

Chapter Sixteen - BEING SELFLESS

There is a very fine line that separates selfishness from selflessness. The one who is selfish is always focused inward upon oneself and what "I" want. The one who is selfless is focused outward toward care and concern for others. What is God's focus? Romans 12:2-3 (NLT) indicates:

> Don't copy the behavior and customs of this world, but let God transform you into a new person by changing the way you think. Then you will learn to know God's will for you, which is good and pleasing and perfect. Because of the privilege and authority God has given me, I give each of you this warning: Don't think you are better than you really are. Be honest in your evaluation of yourselves, measuring yourselves by the faith God has given us.

In his devotional, Insight For Living (January 18, 2021), Charles Swindoll shares the following thoughts about one who is lured into being self-centered:

> I like the tongue in cheek definition of philosophers one of my seminary professors would occasionally use: "Philosophers are people who talk about something they don't understand and then make you think it's your fault!" Lots of philosophies are floating around...Those that are clear enough to be understood usually end up focusing full attention on the individual.

- Education says: Be resourceful; expand yourself!
- Psychology says: Be confident; assert yourself!
- Religion says: Be good; conform yourself!
- Epicureanism says: Be sensuous; enjoy yourself!
- Materialism says: Be satisfied; please yourself!
- Pride says: Be superior; promote yourself!
- Humanism says: Be capable; believe in yourself!
- Philanthropy says: Be generous; release yourself!
- Yourself, yourself, yourself…The cultural emphasis is do something either for yourself, or with yourself, or to yourself.

Does anything on the above list describe who you are or what you are becoming? Obviously, you'll have to make some lifestyle choices. The key is to fit your choices and plans into God's choices and plans for you (Jeremiah 29:11).

The above list falls way short of the focus of one's thought, mind and will towards those of Jesus Christ. His lesson that is often forgotten or ignored is stated in Mark 10:43-45, "Whoever wants to be a leader among you must be your servant, and whoever wants to be first among you must be the slave of everyone else…" His statement is basic: Be a servant! Be ready and willing to give to others!

Charles Swindoll concluded his devotional with this thought: "Let's stop thinking so highly of ourselves, our gifts, our contributions, and our abilities. Stop permitting two strong tendencies, selfishness and conceit, to control you!" He goes on to recommend a reasonable alternative: "Replace selfishness and conceit with humility of mind."

Paul amplifies these thoughts in Ephesians 4:2-3 (NLT),

> Always be humble and gentle. Be patient with each other, making allowance for each other's faults because of your love. Make every effort to keep yourselves united in the Spirit, binding yourselves together with peace.

Similarly, in Philippians 2:1-4 (NLT) he writes to a group of believers who caused him to have great joy and reminds them:

> Don't be selfish; don't try to impress others. Be humble, thinking of others as better than yourselves. Don't look out only for your own interests, but take an interest in others, too.

Horatius Bonar (1857) penned poignant words regarding the wise choice one should make:

> Thy way, not mine, O Lord,
> However dark it be!
> Lead me by Thine own hand,
> Choose out the path for me.
> Smooth let it be or rough,

It will be still the best;
Winding or straight, it leads
Right onward to Thy rest.

Not mine, not mine the choice
In things or great or small;
Be Thou my guide, my strength
My wisdom, and my all…

A valid and subtle emphasis in Bonar's words is that one should make this decision and choice from this day forward. Looking back to what might've been or living in the "if only" realm can cause discouragement and second-guessing. You are being conformed to the image of Jesus and your gifts, talents and function are all part of God's plan for your life. It would be an error to look at where others are, what they have become and what they did to gain their station in life.

Your sole concern should be to pursue the thought, mind and will of Jesus Christ for you! The context of Romans 12 and Ephesians 4 reminds us that the body of Christ, the church, is one and is made up by those whose gifts vary and are being used in different ways. You are not called to duplicate someone else's gifts. You are unique in the mind and will of Jesus Christ. Your focus is to submit who you are to Him and to be used by Him as and how He pleases – where and when He pleases. When that is one's commitment, Jesus Christ will be pleased and all glory will be His.

You have a choice. You can be SELFLESS or SELFISH. Which choice should you make? What choice have you made? To God be the glory, great things He has done – great things He continues to do! Fit your life into His plan and purpose for you! This is the place where you will discover the thought, mind and will of Jesus Christ.

Chapter Seventeen - IN EVERYTING

There are many phrases in Scripture that should cause one pause and assessment. Phrases such as – but God; let us; one another; etc. A verse that has had my attention and has had special meaning lately is Philippians 4:6 (ESV), "In everything by prayer and supplication with thanksgiving let your requests be made known to God." Is anything excluded from God's "everything"? No! Everything includes "all things of any importance or detail."

Another verse that has been rehearsed in my mind is Proverbs 3:6 (ESV), "In all your ways acknowledge him." Is anything excluded from God's "all"? No! All and everything in these verses are inclusive.

A hymn of consecration that is often sung contains the words: "All to Jesus, I surrender; All to Him I freely give; I will ever love and trust Him... I surrender all...All to Thee, my blessed Savior, I surrender all." When we sing these words, is there anything that we deliberately omit in the word "all"? Is there anything that we hold dear that is off -limits to God in our "surrender all" to Him? If so, what do we withhold from Him? Why do we firmly hold onto whatever it is?

An illustration about surrender was shared by F. B. Meyer when he was preaching in Keswick, England (1904):

> I remember so well when He came to my heart and challenged me as to the keys of the fortress...Before I gave them to Him I put one small key in my pocket.

Have not you done that, and handed to Him the bunch minus that key? He gave it back, and said He could not be King at all if He could not be King of everything. I put my hand in my pocket where I had hidden it, and said: I cannot give it, but You may take it, and He took that tiny key. He looked at me with those eyes which are as a flame of fire, and said: Are all the keys there? I said: All but this, and I cannot give it; but I am willing for Thee to take it. He took not just the key but also the entire door. Jesus must have all the keys and access to all of our heart - nothing held back. He must be at the center of our purpose and desire in life.

In everything, we must surrender all to Him. Have you done so? What are you withholding from Him? It will serve us well to consider the context in Philippians 4:4-7 (NKJV). What should be the attitude and action of the follower of Jesus Christ? Answer: "to rejoice in the Lord always." What representative lifestyle should the follower of Jesus Christ display? Answer: "to let your gentleness be known to and by all people." What should other people recognize about you and your life? Answer: that we are "being anxious about nothing." In a world marked by uncertainty and cultural pressures, how can one sustain a life that is free of anxiety? Answer: "by prayer and supplication, with thanksgiving." To whom is one to seek as the object of prayer, supplication and thanksgiving? Answer: "let your requests be made known to God." If that is the genuine commitment and faith objective, how can there be positive and continual result? Answer: By knowing that "the peace of God which surpasses all understanding will guard your hearts and minds through Jesus Christ."

To gain these results in everything that pertains to you and the commitment you have made to the Lord Jesus Christ, there will be a steady unveiling of these qualities – rejoicing, gentleness, calm, peace in your life. They will become a growth pattern as old things pass away and all things become new in one's life. Peter referenced and underscored this continuum of growth in grace when he wrote in Second Peter 1:5-11,

> Giving all diligence, add to your faith virtue, to virtue knowledge, to knowledge self-control, to self-control perseverance, to perseverance godliness, to godliness brotherly kindness, and to brotherly kindness love. For if these things are yours and abound, you will be neither barren nor unfruitful in the knowledge of our Lord Jesus Christ. For he who lacks these things is shortsighted, even to blindness, and has forgotten that he was cleansed from his old sins.

A growth pattern must be obvious to all. Peter goes on to urge us to "be even more diligent to make your call and election sure." Why should this be one's commitment? What benefit will there be when "everything" is part of the pursuit for the mind and will of Jesus Christ? Peter adds: "if you do these things, you will never stumble."

James Perry

When I fear my faith will fail,
Christ will hold me fast...
  For my Savior loves me so,
  He will hold me fast.

Chapter Eighteen - DISPOSITION

What is a disposition? Is it similar to a deposition? No! Well then, how is one to differentiate between the two? Hmmm! A deposition can mean one of two things: (a) the process of giving sworn testimony about actual facts; or (b) a formal statement to be used as evidence in a hearing or court testimony. A disposition usually means: a person's inherent qualities of (a) mind and/or (b) character. For the person pursuing to know the mind and will of Jesus Christ, both deposition and disposition can become important factors.

Historically, both of these words found a place in the actions that occurred December 1955 in Montgomery, Alabama. Rosa Parks had been compliant amid the segregation regulations imposed on African American population in Alabama – until on a busy day and on a crowded bus, Rosa Parks refused to surrender her seat in the last four rows of a bus so that a white person would have a place to be seated. Her disposition had been one of compliance. She went along in order to get along.

What brought about her reaction and change in her disposition? Was this a "straw that broke the camel's back" moment for her? Was it due to a harsh tone in the bus driver's voice and his aggressive manner? Was he sarcastic in his demand? Were the other passengers on the bus becoming engaged in the demand being made of Rosa? Whatever the cause or reason, Rosa made her decision to reject bus driver James F. Blake's "order to vacate her seat in the four rows of seats in the "colored" section of the bus in favor of a white passenger. Such an act of defiance landed Rosa Parks in the Alabama court system. Meanwhile, the African American community boycotted the Montgomery buses for over a year. The prolonged federal judicial lawsuit, Browder v. Gayle, resulted in a November 1956 decision that bus segregation is unconstitutional under the Equal Protection Clause of the 14th Amendment to the United States Constitution. Her disposition made a deposition a necessity.

There are words in a hymn that indicate the timing of when an act of noncompliance can or should take place. The hymn written by James R. Lowell in 1845 states:

> Once to every man and nation,
> Comes the moment to decide,
> In the strife of truth with falsehood,
> For the good or evil side;
> Some great cause, some great decision,
> Offering each the bloom or blight…
>
> it is the brave man chooses
> While the coward stands aside,
> Till the multitude make virtue
> Of the faith they had denied…
>
> Though the cause of evil prosper,
> Yet the truth alone is strong;

Though her portion be the scaffold,
And upon the throne be wrong;
Yet that scaffold sways the future,
And behind the dim unknown,
Standeth God within the shadow,
Keeping watch above His own.

In the first century, Jesus Christ had been a focal point. To eliminate Him as a potential monarch or ruler, He was put to death and the religious community believed they had taken care of their opposition and could move along within the framework of their religious biases. That would've worked well if witnesses hadn't seen Jesus risen from the dead and his subsequent ascension into heaven and if there hadn't been a Day of Pentecost and the response of hundreds of people taking a stand to identify with Jesus Christ and His followers.

The religious leaders of that day decided they would do what they could to eliminate this public message and to silence those who were most vocal and effective. Peter and John were singled out and brought before the religious authorities (Acts 4:1-8, ESV). They were asked one basic question after healing a crippled man (Verse 7): "By what power or by what name did you do this?" One should note the timing of the disposition factor (Verse 13):

> Now when they saw the boldness of Peter and John, and perceived that they were uneducated, common men, they were astonished. And they recognized that they had been with Jesus.

Powerful words – the opponents recognized that these common and uneducated men had been with Jesus. The decision of the opponents was (Verses 18-20): "They called them and charged them not to speak or teach at all in the name of Jesus. But Peter and John answered them: "Whether it is right in the sight of God to listen to you rather than to God, you must judge, or we cannot but speak of what we have seen and heard."

What was their disposition? In the moment where they needed to stand they made a commitment to do so. How would the people respond to the conviction, commitment and disposition of Peter and John? Verses 23-24, 29, 31):

Peter and John went to their friends and reported what the chief priests and the elders had said to them. And when they heard it, they lifted their voices together to God…

And now, Lord, look upon their threats and grant to your servants to continue to speak your word with all boldness…

And when they had prayed, the place in which they were gathered together was shaken, and they were all filled with the Holy Spirit and continued to speak the word of God with boldness.

As you pursue the mind and will of Jesus Christ, what choice have you made for the resistance taking place about the message we are to boldly proclaim? By God's grace, we can remain committed and achieve exploits for Him.

Chapter Nineteen - PERILOUS

For many years, The United States Navy Hymn has included words that describe the uncertainty of the seas. The first stanza references the uncertainty for the sailor:

Eternal Father…
Whose arm hath bound the restless wave,
Who bid'st the mighty ocean deep
Its own appointed limits keep;
O hear us when we cry to thee,
For those in peril on the sea.

Mark 4 references the time when the disciples were steering their ship toward their destination. Jesus was with them but He was sleeping in the stern of the ship. Unexpectedly, a storm raged and the disciples feared they would sink and drown. However, Jesus remained asleep in the stern of the ship. The very idea! Danger surrounding them and Jesus keeps on sleeping! The disciples nearing a point of exhaustion and hopelessness awaken Jesus. Their concern is that Jesus apparently doesn't care about the desperateness of their situation. My mind and heart always go out to the other little boats that were following the larger vessel. Oh, the other little boats were not in the focus of the disciples. Would they capsize? Would they sink? Would the people in their little boats drown? If you were on the larger vessel with the disciples, what would've been your primary concern?

They should've known, even as we should know, Jesus was more concerned that they were thinking like victims rather than believing that with Him they are victors! Jesus speaks three words to them and the perilous waters. "Peace, be still." It's no small wonder that Mary Baker used this situation as the inspiration for a Hymn she composed:

Master, the tempest is raging!
The billows are tossing high!
The sky is overshadowed with blackness,
No shelter or help is nigh;
Carest Thou not that we perish?
How canst Thou lie asleep,
When each moment so madly is threatening
A grave in the angry deep?

There are troubling moments that impact lives in different ways. There is the journal account about the Mayflower voyage and a storm at sea. The historic reference indicates:

John Howland sailed on the Mayflower in 1620 as a manservant of Governor John Carver. Being in the hull of the ship, the noxious (unpleasant odor) and tossing of the ship, necessitated his coming on deck for fresh air. Unexpectedly, Howland was tossed overboard during the storm, and was almost lost at sea. Miraculously, in the darkness, he reached out his hand and managed to grab hold of a dangling sail rope on which he clung tenaciously. Some crew members heard his cries for help and had enough time to utilize a boat-hook to rescue him from the peril of the sea.

His heritage and family tree contains listings of more than one million descendants, some of whom were Presidents George H. W. Bush and George W. Bush. The list also included the wife of President Theodore Roosevelt.

John Howland hanging onto the rope allowed for his life to be spared and his heritage to become a historic reality.

There is a sadder account of the dangers and perils of the sea. Most are familiar with the hymn, It Is Well With My Soul, written by Horatio G. Spafford in 1876. Ira Sankey wrote about the event that inspired the words of that hymn:

> D. L. Moody and I were holding meetings in Edinburgh, in 1874, when we heard the sad news of the loss of the French steamer, Ville de Havre, on her return from America to France,…On board the steamer was a Mrs. Spafford, with her four children. In mid-ocean a collision took place with a large sailing vessel, causing the steamer to sink in half an hour. Nearly all on board were lost. Mrs. Spafford got her children out of their berths and up on deck. On being told that the vessel would soon sink, she knelt down with her children in prayer, asking God that they might be saved if possible; or be made willing to die, if that was His will. In a few minutes the vessel sank to the bottom of the

sea, and the children were lost. One of the sailors of the vessel...while rowing over the spot where the vessel disappeared, discovered Mrs. Spafford floating in the water. When she was able, she cabled to her husband, a lawyer in Chicago, IL: "Saved alone." Mr. Spafford, who was a Christian, had the message framed and hung up in his office. He started for England immediately to bring his wife to Chicago.

When sailing near the spot of the tragedy, the Captain indicated that they were at the spot where his four daughters had drowned. Spafford scratched out some thoughts that became the hymn so many appreciate singing:

When peace, like a river, Attendeth my way,
When sorrows like sea billows roll;
Whatever my lot, Thou has taught me to say,
It is well, it is well, with my soul.

For me, be it Christ, Be it Christ hence to live:
If Jordan above me shall roll,
No pang shall be mine, For in death as in life
Thou wilt whisper Thy peace to my soul.

In Second Timothy 3:1-5 (NKJV), Paul writes about perilous times that are coming. He gives an extended list of how ungodly people will behave during those perilous times:

People will be lovers of themselves, lovers of money, boastful, proud, abusive, disobedient to their parents, ungrateful, unholy, without love, unforgiving, slanderous, without self-control, brutal, not lovers of the good, treacherous, rash, conceited, lovers of pleasure rather than lovers of God - having a form of godliness but denying its power.

During such a time, how will you respond? Will you hear the whisper of Jesus speaking to you and saying: "Peace! Be Still!"? Look to Him! He will hold you securely in His grip!

Let All Who Come Behind You/Us Find You/Us Faithful.

Chapter Twenty - SILENCE

Ecclesiastes 3:1-9 reminds one there is a season and time for everything that transpires in life and the world. One of the instructions (Ecclesiastes 3:7) states: There is "a time to be quiet (silent) and a time to speak." When should one remain silent versus when one should speak? Should the church speak about secular humanism and varying departures from Christian values and foundations or should it continue in its decision to remain silent? Should this question be ignored and treated as rhetorical? Does it have a Biblical response and application?

Proverbs 31:1, 8-9 answers this question with clarity and specificity:

> The sayings of King Lemuel contain this message, which his mother taught him…Speak up for those who cannot speak for themselves; ensure justice for those being crushed. Yes, speak up for the poor and helpless, and see that they get justice.

A telecast from several years ago, Truths That Transform with D. James Kennedy, was shown on January 24, 2021 and included the following:

> Today, 4,000 innocent precious lives of unborn babies were snuffed out… And 300,000 pulpits are silent…

The networks make a mockery of Christians, the Christian faith and Christian values with nearly every show they air… And 300,000 pulpits are silent…

Greed, materialism, violence, sexual immorality are standard fare… And 300,000 pulpits are silent…

Program after program, movie after movie contains anti-Christian episodes and plots… And 300,000 pulpits are silent…

News articles condescendingly refer to the "fundamentalists, right-wing Christians."… And 300,000 pulpits are silent…

Those who speak out for the sacredness of life are branded as extremists…And 300,000 pulpits are silent.

What important matters are being dealt with in our churches? The church bulletin says there will be a meeting to plan the church-wide supper. We are raising money for a new floor cover in the kitchen. (The old one doesn't match the new stove and refrigerator — we must deal with important things first.) The sermon subject last Sunday was "How To Have a Positive Attitude." And best of all — we are organizing a softball team.

Dr. Kennedy's point is that somehow the church has lost sight of the cultural trends and the message the church should be proclaiming for times such as these. What kind of response is usual? "And 300,000 pulpits are silent…"

When Jesus discussed the rational for the separating of goats from sheep (Matthew 25:31-46), a basic fact He shares is that the routine had replaced the primary purpose and mission. The lapse into the routine happened subtly but it became a major factor in Jesus' reminder as to what ministry priorities should be foremost for the average church and Christian. When asked how and when the ordinary or special needs were ignored, the condemning explanation by Jesus to the goats (Matthew 25:44-45) was clear: "I tell you the truth, when you refused to help the least of these my brothers and sisters, you were refusing to help me." The Message paraphrase of these verses is:

> Then those 'goats' are going to say, Master, what are you talking about? When did we ever see you hungry or thirsty or homeless or shivering or sick or in prison and didn't help?
>
> He will answer them, I'm telling the solemn truth: Whenever you failed to do one of these things to someone who was being overlooked or ignored, that was me - you failed to do it to me.

On a personal level, how should one begin to change ordinary behavioral responses to the Biblical ministry Jesus Christ expects from His own? In 1872, Frances R. Havergal wrote a prayer of her own heart that was set to music as a hymn:

> Lord, speak to me that I may speak
> In living echoes of Thy tone;

As Thou has sought, so let me seek
Thine erring children lost and lone.
O use me, Lord, use even me,
Just as Thou wilt, and when, and where,
Until Thy blessed face I see,
Thy rest, Thy joy, Thy glory share.

A favorite prayer hymn is: Speak, Lord, In The Stillness (Emily May Grimes – 1900). From her several stanzas, three address the need (for me) to speak for the Lord:

Speak, O blessed Master,
In this quiet hour;
Let me see Thy face, Lord,
Feel Thy touch of power.

All to Thee is yielded,
I am not my own;
Blissful, glad surrender,
I am Thine alone.

Fill me with the knowledge
Of Thy glorious will;
All Thine own good pleasure
In Thy child fulfill.

May we, the people of God, be bold to speak in the name of the Lord. Be inspired by the words of Acts 4:29-30:

Now, Lord, consider their threats and enable your servants to speak your word with great boldness. Stretch out your hand to heal and perform signs and wonders through the name of your holy servant Jesus.

Ask the Lord to use your life to model Him and your words to speak the good news about Him to those whose lives need to be reached in His name. May all who come behind you/us find that we were faithful regardless of any cost or consequence!

Chapter Twenty-one - COURAGEOUS

Is there a distinction that can be made between one who is courageous and/or one who is known for boldness? To be courageous means: "not being deterred by danger or pain; being brave." Boldness means: "a willingness to take risks and act innovatively; possessing confidence or courage." By contrast, the one who falters or wavers when courage and boldness are called for is seen as displaying cowardice ("lacking bravery, confidence or courage").

It is interesting to observe the time and usage of the word courageous in Scripture. When leadership is transitioning from Moses to Joshua, Moses confers a personal blessing upon Joshua:

> Moses summoned Joshua and said to him in the sight of all Israel: Be strong and courageous, for you shall go with this people into the land that the LORD has sworn to their fathers to give them, and you shall put them in possession of it. It is the LORD who goes before you. He will be with you; he will not leave you or forsake you. Do not fear or be dismayed (Deuteronomy 31:7-8, ESV).

Moses specifies how Joshua is to approach his task: "Be strong and courageous." Moses also specifies the source of all courage and strength: "It is the Lord who goes before you. He will be with you..." Joshua was one of two men who followed the Lord wholeheartedly (Caleb was the other). Both of these men will be responsible in the leadership and settlement of God's people in the Promised Land. Could they be trusted to accomplish their task? Yes! Why? Because they followed the Lord wholeheartedly.

If we fast-forward to events following the Day of Pentecost, ordinary men are representing Jesus before the Jews and Gentiles with courage, strength and boldness. There is a moment when those making any reference to Him will be put to the test by the opponents of Jesus Christ. Acts 4:1-4 records: "...the priests and the captain of the temple and the Sadducees came upon them, greatly annoyed because they were teaching the people and proclaiming in Jesus the resurrection from the dead." They had them arrested because of their courage to speak of Jesus and His resurrection. Acts 4:13 records: "Now when they (the opponents) saw the boldness (courage) of Peter and John, and perceived that they were uneducated, common men, they were astonished."

What does a hostile group do with courageous and boldness? In Acts 4:17-20, they decide they can control this message and movement:

> But in order that it may spread no further among the people, let us warn them to speak no more to anyone in this name. So they called them and charged them not to speak or teach at all in the name of Jesus. But Peter and John answered them: Whether it is right in the sight of God to listen to you rather than to God, you

must judge, for we cannot but speak of what we have seen and heard.

The courage and boldness of Peter and John prevented them from becoming fearful or intimidated by those opposing the message about Jesus Christ. So – what will they do? What will they encourage others to do?

> When they were released, they went to their friends and reported what the chief priests and the elders had said to them. And when they heard it, they lifted their voices together to God and said, "Sovereign Lord…Lord, look upon their threats and grant to your servants to continue to speak your word with all boldness…And when they had prayed, the place in which they were gathered together was shaken, and they were all filled with the Holy Spirit and continued to speak the word of God with boldness (Acts 4:23-31).

There are occasions when discouragement can replace courage and fearlessness. In First Kings 18, we read about the contest between Elijah and the prophets of Baal. With great courage and boldness, Elijah has stated to King Ahab and the 450 prophets of Baal that there is a Living God who can and will destroy man's idols. When Elijah appealed to the throng that had come to see this contest to stand with him, no one stepped forward to identify with God's prophet or with God Himself. The prophet, alone and surrounded by false prophets and a corrupt king, sets the parameters for the contest. The prophets of Baal failed whereas Elijah's God asserts Himself before all. Elijah's confidence, strength, courage and boldness was apparent and triumph was realized. This was First Kings 18. First Kings 19 is totally different. Why? Jezebel, the wife of King Ahab, made a statement that Elijah will not escape her reach and he will die. Suddenly, the confidence, strength, courage and boldness of Elijah vanished and he raced away in fear and a measure of cowardice. He failed to take into account that he could not run away from God. Even though he believed he would be undetected by anyone, First Kings 19:9 indicates: "He came to a cave and lodged in it. And behold, the word of the Lord came to him, and he said to him: What are you doing here, Elijah?"

The Lord has this fearful prophet stand outside of his hiding place. God displays all kinds of His power – strong wind, earthquake, fire – but the Lord was not in any of those things. It was the "low whisper" of God that asked him once again: "What are you doing here, Elijah." The prophet still had work to do for the Lord and was directed to return by the same route and complete his tasks.

Do you seek the "low whispers" of the Lord in and for your life? Or, do you think in terms of spectacular displays? Much is missed if we fail to listen and hear God's whispers. The refrain from an old hymn reminds us about the whispers of God for the troubled and fearful soul:

Whispering hope, oh how welcome thy voice,
Making my heart in its sorrow rejoice.

Be strong and courageous, God is with you and will help you. Boldly stand and speak for Him. Let His strength be your strength! Let His power be your power! This is the only way to know the thoughts, mind and will of Jesus Christ for your life.

Chapter Twenty-two - PERFECT PEACE

Is it possible to find and have peace in a world of unrest and turmoil? In John 14:27 Jesus said:

> Peace I leave with you; my peace I give you. I do not give to you as the world gives. Do not let your hearts be troubled and do not be afraid.

Does the peace Jesus spoken of in John 14:27 represent the calmness of spirit and freedom from anxiety in this century?

And then, when speaking with His disciples, Jesus went on to add in John 16:1, 33 (NLT),

> I have told you these things so that you won't abandon your faith... I have said these things to you, that in me you may have peace. In the world you will have tribulation. But take heart; I have overcome the world.

A broader question emerges in terms of what Jesus meant when He spoke of tribulation in the world. When Paul wrote to Timothy, he indicated there would be dangers and difficult times in the last days. He gave a brief description of what will take place:

> People will love only themselves and their money. They will be boastful and proud, scoffing at God, disobedient to their parents, and ungrateful. They will consider nothing sacred. They will be unloving and

unforgiving; they will slander others and have no self-control. They will be cruel and hate what is good. They will betray their friends, be reckless, be puffed up with pride, and love pleasure rather than God. They will act religious, but they will reject the power that could make them godly. Stay away from people like that! (Second Timothy 3:1-5).

That's a suggestive list of the lurking difficult times and dangers. In Matthew 24, Jesus spoke extensively of the lifestyle people would be living and the things they would prize. In verses 38-39, He then injects these words about Noah's day:

In those days before the flood, the people were enjoying banquets and parties and weddings right up to the time Noah entered his boat. People didn't realize what was going to happen until the flood came and swept them all away. That is the way it will be when the Son of Man comes.

In other words, people jettisoned any concern about God and His Word. They chose to do what they wanted to do when they wanted to do it. They were unconcerned and unaware that a serious God should be taken seriously. These people Jesus spoke of chose to ignore Him and berate anyone who spoke about Him.

The Biblical Christian has been given guidelines and assurances about God's peace. One of these, Philippians 4:6-7 (NLT) should be memorized and posted visibly in one's home.

> Don't worry about anything; instead, pray about everything. Tell God what you need, and thank him for all he has done. Then you will experience God's peace, which exceeds anything we can understand. His peace will guard your hearts and minds as you live in Christ Jesus.

The Amplified Bible expresses verse 7 underscoring the peace one seeks and needs:

> And the peace of God [that peace which reassures the heart, that peace] which transcends all under-standing, [that peace which] stands guard over your hearts and your minds in Christ Jesus [is yours].

Many Funeral Services have included the words of Isaiah 26:3-4, a song of praise to God,

> You will keep in perfect peace all who trust in you, all whose thoughts are fixed on you! Trust in the Lord always, for the Lord God is the eternal Rock.

The Scriptures remind one of a reassuring hymn that asks and answers questions about Peace, Perfect Peace...

- …In this dark world of sin?

The blood of Jesus whispers peace within.

- ,,,By thronging duties pressed?

To do the will of Jesus, this is rest.
- …Death shadowing us and ours?

Jesus has vanquished death & all its powers.
- …Our future all unknown?

Jesus we know, and he is on the throne.
The concluding stanza of the Hymn acclaims:
It is enough: earth's struggles soon shall cease,
and Jesus call us to heaven's perfect peace.

A while back I read a story on social media entitled A Peaceful Prayer about a visiting pastor who attended a men's breakfast in the middle of a rural farming area of the country. The group had asked an older farmer, decked out in bib overalls, to say grace for the morning breakfast.

"Lord, I hate buttermilk", the farmer began. The visiting pastor opened one eye to glance at the farmer and wonder where this was going.

The farmer loudly proclaimed, "Lord, I hate lard." Now the pastor was growing concerned.

Without missing a beat, the farmer continued, "And Lord, you know I don't much care for raw white flour." The pastor once again opened an eye to glance around the room and saw that he wasn't the only one to feel uncomfortable.

Then the farmer added, "But Lord, when you mix them all together and bake them, I do love warm fresh biscuits. So Lord, when things come up that we don't like, when life gets hard, when we don't understand what you're saying to us, help us to just relax and wait until you are done mixing. It will probably be even better than biscuits. Amen.

The person who submitted the above added:
Within A Peaceful Prayer there is great wisdom for all when it comes to complicated situations. Stay strong because our LORD is mixing several things that we don't really care for, but something even better is going to come when HE is done with it.

May the Lord keep and maintain you in the center of His perfect peace. In this special position of refuge, you will soon become more aware of the thoughts, mind and will of Jesus Christ.

Chapter Twenty-three - PURPOSEFUL LIVING

Paul begged a group of Christians to know and have a Biblical purpose for their lives. He begins with Romans 12:1-2 (NLT), "Dear brothers and sisters, I plead with you to give your bodies to God because of all he has done for you." Paul was conveying a sense of urgency and a reason for his plea. The idea is to reflect on the greatness and compassion of God for His people. He adds that mind renewal is needed, "Don't copy the behavior and customs of this world, but let God transform you into a new person by changing the way you think." The way one thinks is amplified throughout Scripture. One brief summary is found in Philippians 4:8,

> Dear brothers and sisters, one final thing. Fix your thoughts on what is true, and honorable, and right, and pure, and lovely, and admirable. Think about things that are excellent and worthy of praise.

This dovetails with the words to the brothers and sisters in Romans 12:2, "Then you will learn to know God's will for you, which is good and pleasing and perfect." These words caused me to give deeper thought to a question I was asked during my first chemo-therapy treatment: "In the past two weeks: Have you ever considered ending your life?" Living was my focus. Suicide was not! I was unprepared to hear that question several more times when I was scheduled for other chemo-therapy infusions.

When I was first told that I was diagnosed as: "Stage 4, Non-Hodgkin's Lymphoma", my thoughts were that my life would be drawing to a close. I thought about it even more seriously because our great grandson (who died at age 8) was not doing well with his treatments for leukemia. But suicide? No! Considering that death could be imminent? Yes!

My thoughts about those questions reoccurred with the news in 2020-2021 that glibly reported: "There has been an increase in suicide rates due to the Covid-19 pandemic; the shelter-in-place mandates; and the shutdown of activities to which many have become accustomed." The news account rarely noted that many suicides were in the younger age group and related to the children being unable to return to the school classroom. There seemed to be little or no purpose to live and the decision was reached to escape it all. Sadly, mind-renewal had not taken place within a major cross-section of people. For the adults, there was the stress about expenses they were incapable of meeting. This was compounded when there was the persistence of no foreseeable light at the end of the pandemic tunnel.

The need for mind-renewal and purposeful living should be a major focus for the Biblical Church in both its message and ministry. Compliance to any government mandate or recommendation should be considered in context of Biblical authority versus secular mandates. Too often, both the Church and the Biblical Christian have succumbed to tunnel vision. Possible secular consequences (of a proclaimed pandemic) are allowed to outweigh valid Biblical principles. As a result, the United States Bill of Rights has been set aside with speculations and suggested solutions based upon the speculations. As a result, many church ministries have been halted. Virtual worship services are the new way to "attend" church. Addressing the framework of coping with cultural trends, the Psalmist was transparent as he shared his inner conflicts and possible solutions. Psalm 73:3-7 (NLT) gives a picture of a troubled-soul and the dangerous path on which it is travelling:

> I almost lost my footing. My feet were slipping, and I was almost gone. I envied the proud when I saw them prosper despite their wickedness. They seem to live such painless lives; their bodies are so healthy and strong. They don't have troubles like other people; they're not plagued with problems like everyone else. They wear pride like a jeweled necklace and clothe themselves with cruelty. They have everything their hearts could ever wish for!

This addresses the frustration and disillusionment one can experience when looking horizontally at life. Is there a need for mind-renewal and an appreciation for purposeful living as one lives vertically? Yes! Is there an overwhelming need to know the mind and will of Jesus Christ for one's life? Yes!

The Psalmist is giving a surface look at what is deemed to be a "successful" and "prosperous" life by the proud and wicked. In doing so, he fails to see the emptiness of the soul. He also fails to consider where life can lead when the prosperity and privilege of "success" is wavering or grave and when one sees no further purpose for living. At that point, some employ suicide as their alternative to life. They really need mind-renewal and transformation!

How did the Psalmist face his concerns? How did he deal with his threshold depression? The answer is

Then I went into your sanctuary, O God, and I finally understood the destiny of the wicked. Truly, you put them on a slippery path and send them sliding over the cliff to destruction (Psalm 73:17-18).

The perception because of his pursuit of the thoughts, mind and will of the Lord enabled the Psalmist to come to the wise decision going forward:

Yet I still belong to you; you hold my right hand. You guide me with your counsel, leading me to a glorious destiny. Whom have I in heaven but you? I desire you more than anything on earth. My health may fail, and my spirit may grow weak, but God remains the strength of my heart; he is mine forever...But as for me, how good it is to be near God! I have made the Sovereign Lord my shelter, and I will tell everyone about the wonderful things you do (Psalm 73:23-27).

These words are the primary sane and focused testimony for a child of God. No matter how severe life can become, God remains the strength of one's heart. He belongs to you and you belong to Him forever! I appreciate the words from a hymn written by William F. Lloyd in 1824:

My times are in Thy hand;
Whatever they may be;
Pleasing or painful, dark or bright,
As best may seem to Thee.

My times are in Thy hand,
I'll always trust in Thee;
And, after death, at Thy right hand
I shall forever be.

Chapter Twenty-four - A RENEWED MIND

How does one gain a renewed mind? What disciplines need to be employed in order to begin to know the mind and will of Jesus Christ? What did Jesus have in mind when He concurred with a response about discipleship that explained: "You must love the Lord your God with all... your mind (Mark 12:30)? How will that dovetail with the cost of discipleship - "those of you who do not give up everything you have cannot be my disciples". (Luke 14:33)?

As previously noted, one must have a renewed mind if one is to determine the good and perfect will of God. Another Biblical instruction is Colossians 3:1-2,

> Since you have been raised to new life with Christ, set your sights on the realities of heaven, where Christ sits in the place of honor at God's right hand. Think about the things of heaven, not the things of earth.

In two devotionals, (January 2021), Charles Swindoll wrote about the mind and the need for change. One insight he offered was:

> Stop allowing the world to be your standard for the way you live and think! Stop being squeezed into that mold! Pursue a radical transformation from within by allowing the Spirit of God to transform your thought pattern.

In Christ, you have no reason whatsoever to keep serving your secular mentality. You have been freed. Gloriously freed! When Jesus Christ truly takes charge of our minds, bringing our every thought captive to Him, we become spiritually invincible. We operate with supernatural power. We walk under God's complete control.

A renewed mind results out of a commitment one makes. There is a deliberate act to divert from horizontal thinking to vertical comprehension. It is a longing and desire to know Jesus Christ more; be conformed to His image more completely; and to make Him known by a lifestyle that is changed and by a spoken word communicating the Good News about Jesus Christ.

An example of a renewed mind and how it can be attained is illustrated by my "Barnabas" friend, Steve Sellers. He shared in a January 2021 post an event that occurred when he was a boy.

His dad was in the USAF and had been stationed in Las Vegas, Nevada. He related that one day they were in the kitchen and his brother was planning to prepare some soup. The room was filled with laughter as they were settling into their new home. However, in less than a split second, laughter turned into anxious tears and desperation. As his brother was preparing soup on the electric stove, something happened that caused him to be shocked and knocked down onto the floor. My brother was laying on the floor lifeless for just a few seconds until CPR and the breath of life was once again in his lungs because of my dad's actions. Then I watched my dad pulling my brother into his arms and doing what a father does, loving on his boy who was once lifeless and now was alive. The desperate tears were now flowing with joy and prayers of Thanksgiving ascended to the Lord.

Why did Steve share this moment in his family's life? He bridges it over to where he is today. Like the suddenness of his brother's electric shock, he received a phone call that had a similar impact. His oncologist's office called to give him recent PET scan results. The report was: "The PET scan showed an uptick in some of the lymph nodes in your chest."

How would Steve respond to this news? How would a home oriented to "a renewed mind" react to an unplanned and unexpected report? Figuratively, the scenario of his brother's experience occurred. He felt as though he had been hit by a jolt of electricity and knocked to the floor. His testimony indicates:

> Then it happened. My Heavenly Father who is always steady and true had me in His arms of grace with the breath of His presence filling my spiritual lungs with air of His peace.

Steve's prayer request is that he and his wife will be upward focused as they find themselves in God's waiting room. Plans one makes for life can be uncertain and suddenly changed. He adds:

> The one thing that is certain is that my Lord loves Me. He is the one who is able to fill my soul (and mind) with His peace even in the midst of the storm. He will embrace me. He will give me His full attention. He will hear each of my tears that fall.

This response is much more than a spiritual theory. It is a factual commitment that keeps one looking to Jesus. He is the Sovereign God. His plans for one's life have been established from before the foundation of the world. It is believing Ephesians 1:4, "Even before he made the world, God loved us and chose us in Christ to be holy and without fault in his eyes." During hard and uncertain times, it is embracing the words of First Peter 1:20-21,

> God chose Jesus Christ as your ransom long before the world began, but now in these last days he has been revealed for your sake. Through Christ you have come to trust in God. And you have placed your faith and hope in God...

A renewed mind does not appear in an emergency moment when a desperate situation arises or when difficult times are marked by questions and few answers. A renewed mind occurs when a commitment has been made to pursue the thoughts, mind and will of Jesus Christ. Steve had the advantage of seeing the principle of trusting that God will do exceeding abundantly above and beyond what one can ask, think or imagine in and for all circumstances (Ephesians 3:20). Steve has clung to Psalm 91 as a place of prayer and refuge. Since the Psalmist speaks of being covered with His feathers and under His wings, one can trust. This is easily attached to Isaiah 40:31,

> But those who trust in the LORD will find new strength. They will soar high on wings like eagles. They will run and not grow weary. They will walk and not faint.

What should you do to gain and live with a renewed mind? The answer is given in Colossians 3:1-2,

> Set your sights (mind) on the realities of heaven, where Christ sits in the place of honor at God's right hand. Think about the things of heaven, not the things of earth.

The songs and prayer of the renewed mind and one's heart can and should be...

> All for Jesus, all for Jesus!
> All my being's ransomed powers:
> All my thoughts and words and doings,
> All my days and all my hours.
>   And
> Turn your eyes upon Jesus,
> Look full in His wonderful face,
> And the things of earth

will grow strangely dim,
In the light of His glory and grace.

Chapter Twenty-five - BEING PRESENT IN HIS PRESENCE

What does it mean to be present in the presence of God? Is this a practice for Sabbath worship or for daily living? Is it a personal or individual attentiveness? Is it a corporate awareness as people gather to worship?

Brother Lawrence, in The Practice of The Presence of God, stated his understanding of being in the presence of God:

> Let us occupy ourselves entirely in knowing God. The more we know Him, the more we will desire to know Him. As love increases with knowledge, the more we know God, the more we will truly love Him. We will learn to love Him equally in times of distress or in times of great joy.
>
> Along with total abandonment must go a complete acceptance of God's will with equanimity and resignation. No matter what troubles and ills come our way, they are to be willingly and indeed joyously endured since they come from God, and God knows what He is doing.

This subject can become complicated in one's thought process. Have some studies and definitions added to the complication? Yes! One example is the Westminster Confession of Faith, Chapter 21. It is an excellent and helpful detailed study. Two of the more basic declarations are Section

2: "Religious worship is to be given to God, the Father, Son, and Holy Ghost; and to Him alone." And, Section 3: "Prayer, with thanksgiving, being one special part of religious worship, is by God required of all men; and, that it may be accepted, it is to be made in the name of the Son, by the help of His Spirit, according to His will, with understanding, reverence, humility, fervency, faith, love, and perseverance; and, if vocal, in a known tongue."

How did Jesus Christ address the subject of worship? Was it possible to keep His statement simple? Yes! While there are additional parts to true worship, the simple statement of Jesus is given in John 4:23-24,

> The time is coming, indeed it's here now, when true worshipers will worship the Father in spirit and in truth. The Father is looking for those who will worship him that way. For God is Spirit, so those who worship him must worship in spirit and in truth.

There are some Biblical occasions where God's presence is dramatically and visibly apparent. Aside from His walking and conversing with Adam and Eve until He removed them from the Garden of Eden, there were several other times when God made Himself visibly known. In Exodus 3:1-6 we read that Moses, at 80 years of age, led a flock of Jethro's to Sinai. Suddenly, a phenomenal event occurs. An angel of the Lord appeared to Moses in a blazing fire from the middle of a bush. It was aflame but not consumed. Moses stared at it in amazement. Moses inched toward the bush to study it.

When the Lord saw Moses approaching, He called to him from the middle of the bush. Moses! Moses! Do not come any closer! Take off your sandals! You are standing on Holy Ground. When Moses heard this, he covered his face because he was afraid to look at God.

He realized he had been and was in the presence of God. Moses would have another face to face encounter of being in the presence of God. This would occur on Mount Sinai, when he received the Ten Commandments written by the finger of God: "When the LORD finished speaking with Moses on Mount Sinai, he gave him the two stone tablets inscribed with the terms of the covenant..." Exodus 31:18.

Isaiah 6 records a very special experience in the life of the prophet Isaiah. It is a time of governmental transition and the need for God's people to hear and learn about the Lord. Isaiah has a personal experience of a vision of heaven and the voice of God. Isaiah sees and hears angel choirs singing in an echoing, cascading way, "Holy, Holy, Holy – the whole earth is filled with His glory." As he experienced this vision of being in the presence of God, it caused him to realize and confess (Verse 5): "I am a sinful man. I have filthy lips, and I live among a people with filthy lips. Yet I have seen the King, the Lord of heaven's armies."

In a similar way, Brother Lawrence shared his sense of being in the presence of God:

> I regard myself as the most wretched of all men, stinking and covered with sores, and as one who has

committed all sorts of crimes against his King. Overcome by remorse, I confess all my wickedness to Him, ask His pardon and abandon myself entirely to Him to do with as He will.

There are other times when God manifests Himself in dramatic ways – Elijah and the contest with the prophets of Baal (First Kings 18); Elisha's servant who was fearful when he saw a massive army amassed against Elisha until his eyes were opened to see God's army (Second Kings 6); the angel appearances to the shepherds and at the birthplace of Jesus (Luke 2). In Matthew 17:1-6 a moment takes place when God manifested Himself in a unique way. Jesus took Peter, James and John up onto a mountain where they could be alone. Suddenly, Moses and Elijah appeared and Jesus conversed with them. God spoke out of a cloud: "This is My beloved Son." After they awoke, the three disciples realized they were in the presence of God.

Hebrews 10:25 directs God's people in terms of worship and the presence of God: "Let us not neglect our meeting together, as some people do, but encourage one another, especially now that the day of his return is drawing near." This verse should be coupled with Psalm 95:6-7 which gives direction of the worship that God deserves and desires. "Come, let us worship and bow down. Let us kneel before the Lord our maker, for he is our God. We are the people he watches over, the flock under his care."

Verse 7 shares a very telling statement: "If only you would listen to His voice today!" Will you be present in the presence of God in your life and worship? Will you listen to His voice? He will be honored if and when you do! Come before Him and worship Him!

> I worship You, Almighty, mighty God,
> There is none like You...
>
> I worship You, O Prince of Peace,
> That is what I want to do.
> I give You praise
> For You are my righteousness...
>
> I worship You, Almighty God,
> There is none like You...

Chapter Twenty-six - STEADFASTNESS

It is a given that as people age, they become less steady than when they were younger. They may stagger or stumble. They may even lose their balance on occasion. This is a reason why it is recommended that older adults avoid climbing on ladders. It is a truism across the spectrum of activities that once were part of the "normal" but now have to be approached cautiously.

When thinking about steadiness and the Biblical Christian life, there are no such prohibitions. To be steadfast is a continuum for those who are pursuing the thoughts, mind and will of Jesus Christ. A verse that should be foremost for all is First Corinthians 15:58, "Be steadfast, immovable, always abounding in the work of the Lord, knowing that your labor is not in vain in the Lord." There are two major thrusts in the text: (1) steadfast, immoveable and (2) always abounding. The NLT paraphrase adds: "Always work enthusiastically for the Lord, for you know that nothing you do for the Lord is ever useless."

What does it mean "to be steadfast"? The clear indication is for one to be: "resolutely or dutifully firm and unwavering." This concept and the word immoveable does not suggest one should be stubborn and insist on one's way. The Biblical Christian must learn to be pliable and develop the lifestyle and ministry commitment as summarized by Paul in First Corinthians 9:19-23,

For though I am free from all, I have made myself a servant to all, that I might win more of them…I have become all things to all people, that by all means I might save some. I do it all for the sake of the gospel, that I may share with them in its blessings.

To be steadfast entails one's awareness of the various people groups one will meet or encounter. If only God's people would have Jesus first and foremost in their minds and wills, it would not only honor Him but enlighten the Biblical Christian. It would also serve to open up practical applications of interaction with real life situations. In a February 2021 Insight devotional, Charles Swindoll reminded his readers about a ministry that is often overlooked: "The next time you witness someone stumbling, be quick to assist them back to their feet. Former stumblers make excellent encouragers." One of the sad side effects of having chemotherapy and taking steroids is that it becomes too easy for one to stumble or fall. Early one morning, I went outside to get some firewood. When I bent over, I lost my balance and fell on the gravel portion of our driveway. I was unable to get myself back up. It was dark and cold. I was alone and helpless. Unexpectedly, my wife had gotten up at 4:00 A.M. and looked for me. She came to my rescue, brought my walker, helped to get me upright and back into the warm home. She has always been steady on her feet but on this occasion she was able to empathize with me and my plight, and epitomized being an encourager. This is a good illustration of what it means to pursue the mind and will of Jesus Christ, especially on behalf of others and their need(s).

It reminded me of the words in Ecclesiastes 4:9-10 (NLT), "Two people are better off than one, for they can help each other succeed. If one person falls, the other can reach out and help. But someone who falls alone is in real trouble." How many people have you observed who have stumbled or are stumbling? Do you reach out to such a one and offer to assist as much as you can? If you do so, do you have the account of The Good Samaritan (Luke 10:29-37) in mind as you provide care and concern?

In our pursuing the mind and will of Jesus Christ, do we incorporate the words of being steadfast, immoveable, always abounding in the work of the Lord when we see one who has stumbled or fallen? Do you think about your effort in terms of "good works" or compassion toward one of the least of these (Matthew 25:31-46)? Do you reckon with the words in James 2:14-17 (ESV),

> What good is it, my brothers, if someone says he has faith but does not have works? Can that faith save him? If a brother or sister is poorly clothed and lacking in daily food, and one of you says to them: Go in peace, be warmed and filled, without giving them the things needed for the body, what good is that? So also faith by itself, if it does not have works, is dead.

The MSG paraphrase expresses:

Do you think you'll get anywhere in this if you learn all the right words but never do anything? Does merely talking about faith indicate that a person really has it? For instance, you come upon an old friend dressed in rags and half-starved and say, "Good morning, friend! Be clothed in Christ! Be filled with the Holy Spirit!" and walk off without providing so much as a coat or a cup of soup—where does that get you? Isn't it obvious that God-talk without God-acts is outrageous nonsense?

What is the Biblical Christian's standard for the faith life and practice? Paul wrote in Second Thessalonians 3:5 (ESV), "May the Lord direct your hearts to the love of God and to the steadfastness of Christ." Second Peter 1:5-8 (ESV) adds,

> Make every effort to supplement your faith with …steadfastness…If this qualitity is yours and is increasing, it will keep you from being ineffective or unfruitful in the knowledge of our Lord Jesus Christ.

A Hymn written by Jan Pinborough (2008) captures the thrust of being steadfast and immoveable.

As the rising generation,
We have learned the gospel plan.
Though the storms of change around us
Challenge faith on every hand.
 Chorus:

Steadfast and immovable,
Standing true unto our Lord;
Looking forward, strong in courage,
Faithful to His glorious word!

Chapter Twenty-seven - UNEXPECTED AWARENESS

No one ever anticipates the unexpected events that occur in one's life experiences. One evening, my wife and I had retired for the night. Lights were out! The television was off! Quietness prevailed! Until – suddenly – unexpectedly – there was a loud BANG. We tried to guess what had happened when just as suddenly – unexpectedly – there was another BANG. I thought it was wise to get up and investigate what was causing the BANG. I entered the kitchen and immediately discovered the unexpected reality – the microwave was smoking and flames were flashing from behind the control panel. By this time, my wife was in the kitchen and had started to remove "stuff" from the cupboard above the microwave so she could unplug it from its power source. At that point the flashing, smoke and flames stopped.

It caused me to think about the spiritually unexpected moments one can and will experience. I have a close friend, Steve, who is having such an unexpected awareness. His lymphoma from seven years ago seems to be showing up again during the routine maintenance examinations. This time it appears to be in his lungs. He wrote me: On my way to see the surgeon. Here's where I have been all morning. (Psalms 34:4-9, 18-19 AMP):

> I sought the LORD [on the authority of His word], and
> He answered me, and delivered me from all my

fears…The angel of the Lord encamps around those who fear Him [with awe-inspired reverence and worship Him with obedience], and He rescues [each of] them. O taste and see that the Lord [our God] is good; How blessed [fortunate, prosperous, and favored by God] is the man who takes refuge in Him. O [reverently] fear the Lord, you His saints (believers, holy ones); for to those who fear Him there is no want. The Lord is near to the heartbroken…many hardships and perplexing circumstances confront the righteous, but the LORD rescues him from them all.

In a follow-up correspondence Steve wrote: "Going to have to do a CT scan to determine the best approach to do the biopsy. I will have that done Monday afternoon." Steve is "the Barnabas" I wrote about in a previous book, The Barnabas Quest. He is a dear brother in Christ whose hope, faith and confidence has been unwavering. Perhaps you know of one who is passing through an unexpected moment. It would be appreciated by that person just to know that you care. Your encouraging word(s) would be timely for the concerned or burden-bearing soul and spirit.

Despite the fact that the disciples had witnessed many powerful ministry events with Jesus, they continually had questions about one thing or another. In Matthew 24:14 (NLT), the disciples were pressing Jesus for a timeline about the kingdom and His return along with the obvious signs that would accompany that return. Jesus gave them a vague but sobering word: "You must be ready all the time, for the Son of Man will come when least expected."

Once again, when Jesus Christ reviewed the seven churches, He gave the summarized and sober words (Revelation 3:3, NLT): "Go back to what you heard and believed at first; hold to it firmly. Repent and turn to me again. If you don't wake up, I will come to you suddenly, as unexpected as a thief."

What is the background that precedes the sobering words of Jesus? Revelation 3:1-2 (NLT) indicates:

> I know all the things you do, and that you have a reputation for being alive but you are dead. Wake up! Strengthen what little remains, for even what is left is almost dead. I find that your actions do not meet the requirements of my God.

What is the cusp (point) that should gain one's positive response? To repent and return to what one first believed. Is it possible that Jesus intends these same sobering words for the "cancel culture" in which we live and serve in the twenty-first century? Yes!

The song in our hearts and minds, one's expectation and awareness should include:

> He is coming again, He is coming again,
> The very same Jesus, rejected of men;
> He is coming again, He is coming again,
> With power and great glory, He is coming again!

O blessed hope! O blissful promise!
Filling our hearts with rapture divine;
O day of days! Hail Thy appearing!
Thy transcendent glory forever shall shine.

We live in a day when the hearts of people are indifferent towards the words and values of the Lord. That is a reality that needs to be faced. The message of hope in scripture is that a Biblical Christian is a victor, not a victim.

Even if the nation and culture has wandered far from the values and standards God revealed in the Holy Scriptures, there is a message of hope to be conveyed. It is not a time for cowardice! It is a day for courage and boldness.

What is the message to be proclaimed to those to whom Christ's return would be unexpected? Obviously, it must be Jesus only, who was crucified, risen and coming again. The song for the hearts and minds of the nation and culture should be:

I've wandered far away from God;
Now I'm coming home;
The paths of sin too long I've trod,
Lord, I'm coming home.

Coming home, coming home,
Nevermore to roam,
Open wide Thine arms of love,
Lord, I'm coming home.

Why is this message of hope significant? Two immediate reasons are: (1) The unexpected moment of death or Christ's return is imminent, and (2) One's health and life expectancy is a variable at best. Life is like a vapor that appears briefly and then vanishes away (James 4:14). Let us pursue the mind and will of Jesus Christ with vigor and commitment. We can also be reminded by the words written by Avis B. Christiansen:

> Only one life to offer
> Jesus, my Lord and King…
> O may it be
> Consecrated alone to Thy matchless glory,
> Yielded fully to Thee.
>
> Only this hour is mine, Lord
> May it be used for Thee…
> Souls all about are dying,
> Dying in sin and shame;
> Help me bring them the message
> of Calvary's redemption,
> In Thy glorious name.
>
> Only one life to offer
> Take it, dear Lord, I pray;
> Nothing from Thee withholding,
> Thy will I now obey…
> Claim this life for Thine own,

to be used, my Savior,
Every moment for Thee.

Chapter Twenty-eight - REMAINING FOCUSED

The blog writer, Dr. D. Clair Davis, a church historian and Professor Emeritus, observes:

> Our culture is very personal, it's all about what this means to me. What that ends up meaning is very negative, there just isn't anything called truth that we all agree on. Being personal is wonderful, but now we're at the brink of not being able to communicate with each other. In the philosophy world that's post-modernism.

Cleon Ochsner, in his book KULAK, recounts that after the Bolshevists had infiltrated Ukraine and began interrogations of the non-compliant, the idea of "truth" was defined by the Bolshevists. The one's being interrogated and persecuted were forced to sign a near blank page that would later be filled in by the Bolshevists indicating their desired results of the personal interrogations.

In our nation, there has been a dominant emphasis on opaque political speech by various candidates. For many of them, their proclamations were either bloviation at best or blatant deceit at worst. Some, even Evangelicals, accepted the deceitful rhetoric. The result of it all, following Election Day, is that the nation will remain as divided (or more divided) as it was before ballots were cast for the most "truth" available.

For the Biblical Christian, how does one remain focused and retain the biblical focus? What must be remembered by the people of God? Daniel had been held captive in Babylon from the time he was a teenager and his ongoing focus was expressed in Daniel 2:21. He received a vision from God that reminded him: "The Lord controls the course of world events; He removes kings and sets up other kings." The godly residents living in nations where an apparent negative-type person is in power face a special challenge. The generation that lived during the 1930s and 1940s know the peril of remaining silent and mostly compliant when the outrageous is occurring. Is remaining silent and compliant the expected and required behavior of the Biblical Christian in the twenty-first century?

What should one do and how should one live when the outrageous and atrocities are taking place? From a purely spiritual commitment, there are guidelines that direct one to remain focused at all times. The scriptures reminded God's faithful people:

Hebrews 12:2, Keep our eyes on Jesus, the champion who initiates and perfects our faith.

Hebrews 13:5, God has said: I will never fail you. I will never abandon you.

Romans 8:28, We know that God causes everything to work together for the good of those who love God and are called according to his purpose for them.

Jeremiah 29:10-11, This is what the LORD says: You will be in Babylon for seventy years. But then I will come and do for you all the good things I have promised and I will bring you home again. For I know the plans I have for you, says the LORD. They are plans for good and not for disaster, to give you a future and a hope.

Some time ago, the Tuscaloosa News, Tuscaloosa, Alabama, contained an editorial by Larry Clayton headlined, "Search For A Christian and Find Truth." Part of his thesis was: "Today... advocates across the university communities of America...preach a message that mixes in race, social justice, sex, gender, and generally create their own truth...to stand as the grand principles of higher education."

Larry Clayton doesn't state a reasonable alternative or his concept of "truth" for higher education. He offers a criticism but no alternative.

In his book, Escape From Reason (Chapter 2), Francis Schaeffer wrote:

It is an important principle to remember, in the contemporary interest in communication and in language study, that the biblical presentation is that though we do not have exhaustive truth, we have from the Bible what I term true truth. In this way we know true truth about God, true truth about man, and something truly about nature. Thus on the basis of the Scriptures, while we do not have exhaustive knowledge, we have true and unified knowledge.

He added:

Within the present culture and that which comes under the banner of acceptability, there is a vagueness about and a loss of truth as it is defined by the Lord and expressed throughout the Holy Scriptures. Your obligation is to be guided by true truth and make Jesus, who declared: I AM the truth, known to all people.

Is there a risk in doing so? Yes! Will you encounter rejection? Yes! Is there a possibility you may experience persecution? Yes! Should these things cause you to change your definition, message and focus? No!

By God's grace, one must remain focused! In a lost world that has basically rejected God and His Word, champions for true truth must have courage to stand and declare that truth clearly and boldly. There are phrases in the hymn, Open Mine Eyes, that should challenge and motivate the Biblical Christian to share the truth. As you purpose to remain focused in your pursuit of knowing the mind and will of Jesus Christ, consider the possibility of these words being a prayer and commitment you make:

Open my eyes, that I may see
Glimpses of truth Thou hast for me…
 Open my ears, that I may hear
Voices of truth Thou sendest clear…
Everything false will disappear.

Open my mouth, and let me bear,

Gladly the warm truth everywhere…

Chapter Twenty-nine - ESCAPING DOLDRUMS

Have you ever had a doldrum-moment? Do you know of anyone who lives in the doldrums realm? What is a doldrum? It seems to be one of the catch-all words in our language. For the merchant seaman, it refers to: "A belt of calm and light baffling winds north of the equator between the northern and southern trade winds in the Atlantic and Pacific Oceans." A more general meaning is: "A state of inactivity or stagnation, as in business or art." The basic meaning for the way the term is used is: "A dull, listless, depressed mood; low spirits."

The broad question is whether or not a Biblical Christian who is seeking the mind and will of Jesus Christ can be in a doldrum state of mind. There are times when experiences can be confusing and discouraging. Psalm 73:2-3 (NLT) is written by Asaph. In the midst of being downcast and discouraged, Asaph cries out to God in his personal despair: "But as for me, I almost lost my footing. My feet were slipping, and I was almost gone. For I envied the proud when I saw them prosper despite their wickedness." Obviously, this is a depressed mood and one who is in low spirits. He adds in Verse 16, "I tried to understand why the wicked prosper. But what a difficult task it is!" He seems so alone and desperate. He is wondering what purpose is there to the godly life when the ungodly are prospering. He sees them enjoying ease and luxury.

There was another occasion when Elijah (I Kings 18) has been very effective in his opposition to and contest with the prophets of Baal. In the name of the Lord, he has divine power to intervene in His name and prevail. It is at this point that the people realize that the Lord really is the omnipotent God. This is true for Elijah in I Kings 18. When we come to I Kings 19, we learn that Ahab's wife, Jezebel. has threatened Elijah's demise and death. From the peak of exhilaration of seeing God's power shattering the influence of the prophets of Baal, he quickly descends into a "slough of despond" (reference to a swamp in Pilgrim's Progress). He became fearful, discouraged and despairing for his life. He makes the decision to flee as far away as possible to escape Jezebel's threat and determination to kill him. He is a man with a doldrum-moment.

He runs 40 days and nights (many miles) until he comes to Mount Sinai, finds a cave and takes refuge in it. No one will know where he went or be able to find him. Suddenly, someone who does know where he is calls him out by name (First Kings 19:9 NLT): "What are you doing here, Elijah?" His doldrum reason given is:

I have zealously served the LORD God Almighty. But the people of Israel have broken their covenant with you, torn down your altars, and killed every one of your prophets. I am the only one left, and now they are trying to kill me, too.

Is Elijah correct in his assessment of prevailing conditions? No! The Lord has Elijah come to the mouth of the cave and responds to him in various ways in Verses 11-12,

> As Elijah stood there, the Lord passed by, and a mighty windstorm hit the mountain. It was such a terrible blast that the rocks were torn loose, but the Lord was not in the wind. After the wind there was an earthquake, but the Lord was not in the earthquake. And after the earthquake there was a fire, but the Lord was not in the fire. And after the fire there was the sound of a gentle whisper.

It is in the gentle whisper that Elijah hears the Lord's soul-searching question once again: "What are you doing here, Elijah?" In verses 15-16, the Lord instructs Elijah to return by the way he came. There is work that he has left undone. The Lord also adds in verse 19, by the way, Elijah, I have preserved 7,000 faithful prophets who have not bowed their knee to Baal nor kissed him. Along with the doldrums, there is always the danger of miscalculation.

Every once in a while in some format, someone will post a doldrum moment when they indicate: I am so lonely. In this day when the Covid-19 pandemic dominates several nations, shelter-in--place directives and mask mandates have been issued, there are multitudes of people who through no fault of their own have become isolated. This is true for those who are in a nursing home or retirement center; for a patient in a hospital where a no-visitor policy was being implemented;

or the older person who lives alone (or with a spouse) but who does not receive a phone call or visit from a family member or close friend. These and other examples all feed into the doldrums syndrome that exists and prevails.

Jesus may have had this in mind when He stated (Matthew 11:28 - NLT); "Come to me, all of you who are weary and carry heavy burdens, and I will give you rest." Or as the Message states: "Are you tired? Worn out? Burned out...? Come to me. Get away with me and you'll recover your life. I'll show you how to take a real rest."

When Moses gave his farewell words to the people, he called Joshua out by name and reminded him (Deuteronomy 31:7-8): "Be strong and courageous...The Lord himself goes before you and will be with you; He will never leave you nor forsake you. Do not be afraid; do not be discouraged." The key words are for one who may face "doldrums" (or discouragement), "the Lord will never leave or forsake you."

Do you know someone who is struggling with doldrums? What role should you have with such a one? Hebrews 10:22-25 (MSG) mandates: "Let's keep a firm grip on the promises that keep us going. He (the Lord) always keeps his word. Let's see how inventive we can be in encouraging love and helping out each other... (especially one who is experiencing a period of doldrum-itis)."A chorus reminds any "doldrum-oriented person" - - -

Down in the dumps I'll never go,
That's where the devil keeps me low,
So, I'll sing with all my might,

And I'll keep my armor bright,
But, down in the dumps I'll never go.

An evangelist from another generation would sometimes inject into his sermon a song he had learned as a boy:

Cheer up ye saints of God,
There's nothing to worry about;
Nothing to make you feel afraid,
Nothing to make you doubt;
Remember Jesus never fails;
So why not trust him and shout,
You'll be sorry you worried at all,
tomorrow morning.

The person who has plunged into the doldrums has allowed consideration of the circumstances rather than looking to the Lord who has proven He is victorious in anything that may infiltrate one's life. The words of Colossians 3:1-2 should govern who one is and what the Lord expects one to be. If the Biblical Christian is seriously pursuing the mind and will of Jesus Christ, God will prove to be a viable refuge and fortress. One should always, with joyfulness and gratitude, recall:

The Lord's our Rock, in Him we hide,
A Shelter in the time of storm;
Secure whatever ill betide,
A Shelter in the time of storm.

Chapter Thirty - GOBSMACKED

At some point in your life, you have probably been gobsmacked (astonished, astounded). You may not have realized it but intuitively or innately you have experienced it. You have observed something unimaginable and/or repulsive as it happened. What is it to be gobsmacked? It is a word of British origin meaning: "to be utterly astonished; astounded." A sentence or two illustrate how it was and is being used; "There are times when you run out of words to describe the actions of local politicians, you are sometimes left gobsmacked by the sheer audacity of their decisions." Or, "There are still some things in life which leave me utterly gobsmacked."

There are also situations in the Bible where being gobsmacked is described and illustrated. First Kings 9:8, "This temple will become a pile of ruins. Everyone who passes by it will be so gobsmacked that they will ask: Why did the Lord do this to this land and to this temple?" Isaiah 29:9, "Be gobsmacked, blind yourselves and be blind! They are drunken, but not with wine; they stagger, but not with strong drink." One additional reference, Jeremiah 4:9, "On that day, declares the Lord, the courage of the king and the leaders will fail. The priests will be gobsmacked and the prophets gobsmacked as well."

How is gobsmacked applied in the Scripture references? In First Kings 9, the word is: "astounded." In

Isaiah 29, the usage is: "astounded and astonished." In Jeremiah 4, the application is: "appalled and astonished." The New Testament has several places where being gobsmacked is implied. Acts 2:7, on the Day of Pentecost, the response by the listening crowds was: "And they were gobsmacked, astounded and amazed saying: Look! Aren't all these who are speaking (in various known languages) Galileans?"

Gobsmacked originated in 1980. It expressed: "being shocked by a blow to the mouth, or to clapping a hand to one's mouth in astonishment." Today it could be used in reference to the recent political actions and presidential choice. The fact that many evangelicals were willing to compromise their biblical values by choosing change in the government left many gobsmacked by the vote cast and the choice made.

Despite what may prove to be a disaster, there is a given reality for the Biblical Christian amid the pending chaos. Daniel 2:20-22 (NLT) reminds us our true value and true confidence. "Daniel said,

> Praise the name of God forever and ever, for he has all wisdom and power. He, God, controls the course of world events; He removes kings and sets up other kings. He gives wisdom to the wise and knowledge to the scholars. He reveals deep and mysterious things and knows what lies hidden in darkness, though he is surrounded by light…

There is an inescapable truth the Biblical Christian should embrace in times with many unknowns and that is to be biblically gobsmacked by remembering who God is and by knowing the mind and will of Jesus Christ. Ephesians 3:20 establishes that God "…is able to do far more abundantly than all that we ask or think, according to the power at work within us…" This same truth about God is stated in Second Peter 1:3-4 (ESV),

> His divine power has granted to us all things that pertain to life and godliness, through the knowledge of him who called us to his own glory and excellence, by which he has granted to us his precious and very great promises, so that through them you may become partakers of the divine nature…

A hymn that serves as a testimony for the Biblical Christian was written by Charles Gabriel in 1898,

> I stand amazed in the presence
> Of Jesus the Nazarene,
> And wonder how He could love me,
> A sinner, condemned, unclean.

Another hymn he wrote that expresses a similar thought and serves as an expression of spiritual growth is:

> I stand all amazed at the love Jesus offers me,
> Confused at the grace that so fully
> He proffers me;
> I tremble to know that for me
> He was crucified,
> That for me, a sinner,

He suffered, He bled, and died.

The refrain serves as a heart-felt response to both hymns that focus on the amazing grace of the amazing Lord:

Oh, it is wonderful that

He should care for me!

Enough to die for me!

Oh, it is wonderful,

wonderful to me!

In the pursuit of knowing the mind and will of God, the things of this life and world need to be blocked out. One's focus has to be on knowing the Lord and His perfect will for one's life. The words in the hymn written by Edward H. Bickersleth, Jr. (1875) express the approach for learning what the will of the Lord means for one's personal spiritual journey and the expectation that one will do it. In doing so, there will be the personal conviction and realization that:

Peace, perfect peace,

by thronging duties pressed?

To do the will of Jesus, this is rest.

Chapter Thirty-one - FAILURE IS NOT FINAL

There are references in the Holy Scriptures that share insights into the lives of people who made poor choices and experienced the overwhelming sense of uselessness and failure. Failure does not have to be the final destination for a Biblical Christian. If one chooses to be focused and dwell upon negative decisions one has made, then the sense of failure will be one's experience.

There is an interesting moment recorded in Matthew 17:2-3. Jesus has taken Peter, James and John to go with Him on a six day journey to be alone on a nearby mountain. While they are there, a heavenly intervention occurs. (Jesus) "…was transfigured (becoming something more beautiful and elevated) before them. His face shone like the sun, and His clothes became as white as the light. And behold, Moses and Elijah appeared to them, talking with Him." What did they speak about? Luke gives us a brief glimpse into their conversation, Luke 9:28-33 (NKJV),

> (Jesus) …took Peter, John, and James and went up on the mountain to pray. As He prayed, the appearance of His face was altered, and His robe became white and glistening. And behold, two men talked with Him, who were Moses and Elijah, who appeared in glory and spoke of His

decease which He was about to accomplish at Jerusalem.

Why were Peter, James and John present on that mountain? What were they supposed to witness and understand? Why is it that when Jesus takes His followers to special moments, we find them weary and falling asleep? Luke takes note of this,

> Peter and those with him (James and John) were heavy with sleep; and when they were fully awake, they saw His glory and the two men who stood with Him.

What had they missed? What had they failed to hear? What would be the immediate action they should take? What moment would they continue to be unaware of in the life of Jesus Christ? Peter's idea…

> Then it happened, as Moses and Elijah were parting from Him, that Peter said to Jesus: Master, it is good for us to be here; and let us make three tabernacles: one for You, one for Moses, and one for Elijah.

They weren't with Jesus to witness the glory of heaven displayed or to have a vision of Moses and Elijah. They slept through the important reference to the death and suffering that Jesus would shortly undergo in Jerusalem. The comment of Luke about Peter's idea to build three tabernacles is summarized, "…not knowing what had been said." Much as they had done in the Garden of Gethsemane when Jesus had intently prayed, they slept through the crucial words about the suffering and death of Jesus Christ.

What about this scene represents the possibility of the potential for failure? Most commentaries share that the appearance of Moses was to represent The Law, whereas the appearance of Elijah was to represent the Prophets. That is true, but there is another lesson to be understood.

Moses spent forty years in Pharaoh's household. He was able to enjoy all of the benefits that were available to Pharaoh while he was there. Moses spent the next forty years in the desert as part of Jethro's household in Midian after he fled from Pharaoh's jurisdiction because he had murdered and buried an Egyptian. At eighty years of age, Moses learned to be a shepherd and had led Jethro's flock to the back of the desert (Exodus 3).

While there, Moses witnessed a burning bush that was not being consumed. As he drew near to it, God spoke to him and indicated he was standing on holy ground. At eighty years of age, God now wants to take one whose life had been marked by failure and have him appear before Pharaoh to gain the release of approximately two million of God's captive people. In Exodus 3:13, God indicated who he was to represent and how he should make known the living God. Moses was to make known that "I AM WHO I AM" had sent him to appeal to Pharaoh to let His people go!

The uniqueness is that Moses who had been fearful and sensing uselessness is now being entrusted with God's message and the responsibility to lead God's people to the

Promised Land. Moses will be able to move from failure to success if he goes in the name and power of Almighty God. Moses will lead God's people across the desert to the threshold of the Promised Land at Kadesh-Barnea. But because of his past indignation and anger toward God's people at Marah and his striking the rock to get them water, he was found to be unfit to continue into the Promised Land. Why? Because he acted on his own rather than continuing to do what God wanted done when it needed to be done. The Lord will take Moses up onto a mountain and allow him to see the Promised Land and soon thereafter he will be buried in a place that only God knows.

Elijah is a different situation. He has followed the Lord during hard and dangerous times. He has witnessed the power of God. He has stood before King Ahab and the four-hundred-fifty prophets of Baal. He has called upon God's power to be displayed and God answered. After that great event on Mount Carmel (First Kings 18), Elijah becomes fearful and certain of imminent death because of the spoken words of Jezebel, the wife of King Ahab (First Kings 19).

Elijah will flee because of the Jezebel's threat and journey forty days to escape her wrath. He comes to a mountain and finds refuge in a cave. He feels safe and secure there until he hears the voice of God calling: "What are you doing here, Elijah?"

There is a similarity between Moses and Elijah. Both men have heard the voice of God. Both men will have a personal moment with God on Mount Sinai – Moses to have the finger of God inscribe His Law for His people, and Elijah to hear the whisper of God to return the way he had come and finish his God-appointed tasks, ministry and message. What both men had considered to be their failure, was not final for them. God intervened in their lives to have them pursue the mind and will of the Lord and to carry out His assignments for them.

The same truth is valid for us. God is not done with us yet. What we consider to be our failures do not need to define who we are or how God will use us. Our failures do not need to be final. What is it that you have left undone because you believe you are a failure and should no longer be entrusted with God's tasks? If your failure is final, you will be relegated to a cemetery. If your failure is a stepping stone toward success, God will show you the way and enable you to complete the assignments He has designated for you to do. Our prayer should always be: "Lord, make me Your instrument that You can and will use for Your own glory! An appropriate hymn expresses what our commitment, response and readiness should be to our Lord,

His faithful follower I would be,
For by His hand He leadeth me.

Chapter Thirty-two - REFLECTIONS

When we considered failure is not final, we noted there were two sets of three individuals. Peter, James and John were brought by Jesus Christ. After arrival on the mountain, Jesus Christ is transfigured and there is an appearance of Moses and Elijah with Him. We know what Jesus was doing – speaking with Moses and Elijah about His approaching death (Luke 9:28-36). In this same passage, we discover what Peter, James and John were doing! They were asleep just as they would be later in the Garden of Gethsemane (Matthew 26:36-38). Instead of watching in prayer with Jesus, their weariness overcame them and they fell asleep, not just once but three times.

Scripture instructs that one is to pray continually and pray about everything. Are Biblical Christians today any different than Peter, James and John were during the crucial moments Jesus experienced as His death was near? What was central in the mind of Jesus Christ? Had He clearly indicated His sense of urgency with them? In Matthew 26:36-38, Jesus was with Peter, James and John in "the olive grove called Gethsemane and he asks them to sit here while he went over there to pray. He became anguished and distressed and told them: "My soul is crushed with grief to the point of death. Stay here and keep watch with me." Did the disciples feel compelled to display concern or empathy regarding the details of what He was about to pray? Obviously, Not! They could not and did not stay awake. They were unprepared for the impending arrest and all that followed as Jesus was approaching the cross to die. It is safe to assume the disciples sat down and were as comfortable as possible. Whether it was boredom or weariness, on both occasions, they slept. At the very least, it left them ignorant about the intensity of Jesus praying in the garden and the conversation on the Mount of Transfiguration. The will of God and the imminence of death were the issues being pondered (See: Luke 9:28-32). Needless to say, the disciples missed the crucial elements of the prayer and discussion. Result? They were unprepared and fled from Jesus so they would not be killed along with Him.

Many times we find ourselves tempted to suggest that eternal matters are a surprise to us. Surprise(s) because we have become weary in watching and waiting patiently for the Lord's timing and His disclosing His will. There is a passage where the tables could be turned. In Mark 4, the disciples have struggled to keep their boat afloat amid a fierce storm. On this occasion, they ultimately appeal to Jesus who was asleep in the stern of the boat. What are their words to Jesus at their crucial moment? "Master, don't you care that we are perishing?" Wow! Just shift now to the garden and mountain when they were asleep. Could Jesus have justifiably said to them: "Don't you care that I am about to die for the perishing souls of mankind?"

In the February 15, 2021 devotional, Insight For Living by Charles Swindoll, he writes about some of the various surprises in the Bible. He asked: "Have you ever traced the surprises through the Bible? That book is full of them."

Like when Adam and Eve stumbled upon Abel's fresh grave.

When Enoch's footprints stopped abruptly.

When Noah's neighbors first realized it wasn't simply sprinkling.

When Moses heard words from a bush that wouldn't stop burning.

When Pharaoh's wife screamed: Our son is dead!

When manna first fell from the sky.

When water first ran from the rock.

When a ruddy runt named David whipped a rugged warrior named Goliath.

When a judge named Samson said yes instead of no. When a prophet named Jonah said no instead of yes. When the disciples discovered that Judas was the one.

When the only perfect One who ever lived died on a criminal's cross.

When Mary saw Him through the fog that epochal Sunday morning.

He goes on to write there are many more similar instances that are seen as surprises that might not have been if His followers were attentive in prayer and in application of His Word. Their failure would not be final. Acts 1:8 indicates they will receive Holy Ghost power and be able to achieve exploits for Jesus Christ. Even though Peter denied knowing Jesus Christ, the power of the Holy Ghost enables him to become the primary spokesman on the Day of Pentecost. James will be a chief spokesman in the council of Jerusalem (Acts 15). John will go on to write in his letters about the love of God in Christ (more than 75 times in First John).

All of us have had moments of failure in our Christian walk and spiritual journey. There are two options. One can surrender to one's failures and become spiritually impotent; or one can pursue the mind and will of Jesus Christ for one's life. Failure is only final if one surrenders to the circumstances of life and rejects the divine transformative power of Jesus Christ. We should never forget Second Corinthians 5:17, "Anyone who belongs to Jesus Christ has become a new person. The old life is gone; a new life has begun!" Is this a choice you have made? Is this what you have appropriated and committed yourself to be and do? Don't delay in making this commitment your commitment. Then, make the words of a simple gospel song your daily words expressing your commitment. The song is an Indian folk tune that was used with the lyrics written by Sundar Singh in the early 1900s. Do the words represent the commitment of your life:

I have decided to follow Jesus...No turning back?

The world behind me, the cross before me...No turning back?

Though none go with me, I still will follow...No turning back?

Will you decide now to follow Jesus...No turning back?

Chapter Thirty-three - VICTORY IS AVAILABLE

Victory is not only available, it is also achievable. The idea of victory is common within and throughout the culture. When Vince Lombardi was head football coach with the Green Bay Packers (1959-1967), he was known for his philosophy of life for a football player. He is noted for his sayings about teamwork:

> The achievements of an organization are the results of the combined effort of each individual. People who work together will win, whether it be against complex football defenses, or the problems of modern society. Individual commitment to a group effort – that is what makes a team work, a company work, a society work, a civilization work.

His most famous motivational statement was: "Winning is not a sometime thing, it is an all the time thing. You don't do things right once in a while…you do them right all the time."

What if we branched from Lombardi's motivational philosophy and applied it to the Biblical Church and Biblical Christian? Would the Church and the Christian view victory as being just available for both or intended for both to pursue the mind and will of Jesus Christ and realize victory is achievable and attainable. This would be the test for Peter, James and

John (as well as the other disciples). They had to face their need for behavioral transformation and gaining personal discipline for life and ministry. If they remembered what Jesus had instructed them: "I have given you an example to follow. Do as I have done to you...Now that you know these things, God will bless you for doing them" (John 13:15-17).

How does one arrive at this point of following the example of Jesus Christ? Several starting places are:

Psalm 37:5-7 – "Commit your way to the Lord, trust also in Him...Rest in the Lord, and wait patiently for Him."

Proverbs 3:5-6 – "Trust in the Lord with all your heart, and lean not on your own understanding; in all your ways acknowledge Him, and He shall direct your paths."

Proverbs 16:3 – "Commit your works to the Lord, and your thoughts will be established."

Joshua 22:5 – "Take careful heed to do the commandment and the law which Moses...commanded you, to love the Lord your God, to walk in all His ways, to keep His commandments, to hold fast to Him, and to serve Him with all your heart and with all your soul."

Luke 14:25-33 – The cost of discipleship equals total and complete commitment to Jesus Christ – "If you want to be my disciple, you must, by comparison, hate everyone else... otherwise you cannot be my disciple... If you do not carry your own cross and follow me, you cannot be my disciple... And - you cannot become my disciple without giving up everything you own."

There are any number of passages that address the needed discipline and commitment if one is to know the reality of victory in one's life. When I first enrolled in a bible college, there was an emphasis on the victorious Christian life. Occasionally, there would be guest speakers who were part of the Keswick Movement which began in England. Some of the reiterated and adopted goals of the movement include an emphases on: "The lordship of Christ in personal and corporate living; Life transformation through the fullness of the Holy Spirit; Evangelism and missions world-wide; and discipleship and training of people of all ages."

The founding president of the bible college, Dr. Robert McQuilkin, wrote some of his thoughts in a book, Always In Triumph. One of the key verses he mentioned that resonated with me then and now is Second Corinthians 2:14 (NKJV), "Now thanks be to God who always leads us in triumph in Christ, and through us diffuses (across a wide area and to many people) the fragrance of His knowledge in every place." It is no wonder that the bible college chose as its mission statement for the students: "To know Him and to make Him known." Along with that was the theme hymn, All For Jesus.

All for Jesus, all for Jesus!

All my being's ransomed powers:

All my thoughts and words and doings,

All my days and all my hours.

Let my hands perform His bidding,
Let my feet run in His ways;
Let my eyes see Jesus only,
Let my lips speak forth His praise.

Would the disciples learn these truths and live transformed lives following the ascension of Jesus Christ? The answer is – Yes! For the cause of Jesus Christ and His gospel, Peter, James and John suffered considerably. Peter was crucified around 66 AD in Rome under the persecution of Emperor Nero. James was the first of the 12 to be put to death. King Herod had him killed by the sword in Jerusalem (Acts 12). John, the writer of the Gospel of John, the book of the Revelation and three epistles bearing his name is the only one of the 12 that history says was not put to death for his faith, although he suffered greatly while isolated on the Isle of Patmos.

The apostle Paul shared his testimony of suffering in Second Corinthians 11:16-23.

I have worked much harder, been in prison more frequently, been flogged more severely, and been exposed to death again and again. Five times I received from the Jews the forty lashes minus one. Three times I was beaten with rods, once I was pelted with stones, three times I was shipwrecked, I spent a night and a day in the open sea, I have been constantly on the move. I have been in danger from rivers, in danger from bandits, in danger from my fellow Jews, in danger from Gentiles; in danger in the city, in danger in the country, in danger at sea; and in danger from false believers. I have labored and toiled and have often gone without sleep; I have known hunger and thirst and have often gone without food; I have been cold and naked.

Despite all of that, he was glad to share his personal commitment in Galatians 2:20 (NLT), "My old self has been crucified with Christ. It is no longer I who live, but Christ lives in me. So I live in this earthly body by trusting in the Son of God, who loved me and gave himself for me."

In reading the various scriptures referencing disciplines for the godly life; being Spirit-filled; committing who I am and what I have; following the example of Jesus Christ and practical ministry – it leaves one with a sense of a greater consecration to the great and loving Savior.

When looking at the first century servants of the Lord and what they endured to not only know Christ but to make Him known, the words of a hymn, Am I a Soldier of the Cross, swirl through my mind...

Must I be carried to the skies
On flowery beds of ease,
While others fought to win the prize,
And sailed through bloody seas?

Are there no foes for me to face?
Must I not stem the flood?
Is this vile world a friend to grace,
To help me on to God?

Victory in Jesus Christ is achievable and attainable. Our lives can be lived always in triumph as we implement Hebrews 12:14 (NLT), "…work at living a holy life, for those who are not holy will not see the Lord." This is our pathway as we pursue to know the mind and will of Jesus Christ for our lives. He is worth knowing and worthy to be properly represented by us in this world and culture.

Can you be counted upon as you decide to be wholly committed to Him and being eager to follow Him regardless of personal cost? Will the theme of your life be to know him; to make Him known; and to train (disciple) others who will want to know and to make Him known?

May the reality and song of your heart and life be Psalm 63:3-5,

Your unfailing love is better than life itself; how I praise you! I will praise you as long as I live, lifting up my hands to you in prayer. You satisfy me more than the richest feast. I will praise you with songs of joy.

EPILOGUE

Pursuing the mind and will of Jesus Christ requires discipline and commitment. It takes seriously the words of Jesus in Matthew 5:6 (ESV), "Blessed are those who hunger and thirst for righteousness, for they shall be satisfied." The Amplified Bible translation of this verse is: "Nourished by God's goodness are those who hunger and thirst for righteousness - those who actively seek right standing with God - for they will be completely satisfied." A discipline and commitment to begin and maintain a spiritual diet, hungering and thirsting after God's righteousness, is not easy.

Some of the Biblical disciplines and values are: "Seek first the kingdom of God and His righteousness" (Matthew 6:33). "Those who seek me diligently find me..." (Proverbs 8:17). David's prayer (Psalm 63:1 NIV), "You, God, are my God, earnestly I seek you; I thirst for you, my whole being longs for you..." The prophet Isaiah urges: "Seek the Lord while he may be found; call upon him while he is near..." (Isaiah 55:6 ESV). A reason for seeking the Lord is given in Verse 8: (Because) "...My thoughts are not your thoughts, neither are your ways My ways, declares the Lord." An emphasis is also given in terms of the Biblical Christian's relationship to Jesus Christ. Jesus stated in John 10:27, "My sheep hear my voice, and I know them, and they follow Me."

The prayer of Epaphras, Colossians 4:12 should be personalized and referred to frequently, "Epaphras...(is) always struggling on your behalf in his prayers, that you may stand mature and fully assured in all the will of God." In The Message, John Peterson paraphrases this verse: (Epaphras) "He's been tireless in his prayers for you, praying that you'll stand firm, mature and confident in everything God wants you to do (and be)."

Some words from hymns address one's need to remember the prevailing relationship with Jesus Christ. It is best acknowledged by those who hear, heed and follow Him.

> Jesus calls me; I must follow,
> Follow Him today…

> Jesus calls me ; I must follow,
> Follow every hour,
> Know the blessing of His presence,
> Fullness of His power.

Refrain:

> Follow, I will follow Thee, my Lord,
> Follow every passing day;
> My tomorrows are all known to Thee,
> Thou wilt lead me all the way.

Another hymn expresses a similar urgency that disallows excuses or inconveniences to limit one's desire to pursue the mind and will of Jesus Christ. Two stanzas express what some of those inconveniences may be,

> In our joys and in our sorrows,
> Days of toil and hours of ease,

Still He calls, in cares and pleasures,
Christian, love Me more than these!

Jesus calls us! By Thy mercies,
Savior may we hear Thy call,
Give our hearts to Thine obedience,
Serve and love Thee best of all.

How can the child of God pursue Jesus Christ's will and mind with discipline and commitment? If limitations seem to be overwhelming, and one feels inadequate, what words of God can motivate one to press on in following Jesus Christ? When Paul prayed three times asking the Lord to remove his thorn in his flesh, the request went unanswered. Instead, the Lord reminded Paul, "My grace is sufficient for you, for my power is made perfect in weakness" (Second Corinthians 12:8). Do you believe that same truth applies to you?

Paul's perspective on life's goals and purposes is given in Second Corinthians 4:7-10,

> We have this treasure in jars of clay, to show that the surpassing power belongs to God and not to us. We are afflicted in every way, but not crushed; perplexed, but not driven to despair; persecuted, but not forsaken; struck down, but not destroyed; always carrying in the body the death of Jesus, so that the life of Jesus may also be manifested in our bodies.

As the Biblical Christian pursues the mind and will of Jesus Christ, the challenges of life should not deter one's motivation and purpose to know Jesus Christ more completely; to serve Him more vigorously; to make Him known to more people; and to thank Him for the privilege He has granted to allow you and me to serve Him.

Paul shares in Philippians 2:25-30 a level of discipline and commitment by Epaphroditus to follow Jesus Christ regardless of personal challenges or costs,

> I have thought it necessary to send to you Epaphroditus my brother and fellow worker and fellow soldier, and your messenger and minister to my need, for he has been longing for you all and has been distressed because you heard that he was ill. Indeed he was ill, near to death. But God had mercy on him, and not only on him but on me also, lest I should have sorrow upon sorrow. I am the more eager to send him, therefore, that you may rejoice at seeing him again, and that I may be less anxious. So receive him in the Lord with all joy, and honor such men, for he nearly died for the work of Christ, risking his life to complete what was lacking in your service to me.

May the tribe of Epaphroditus increase and may we be found as disciplined and committed in our pursuit of the mind and will of Jesus Christ.

About the Author

James Perry has served the Church with more than 54 years of continuous ministry. He attended Columbia Bible College (now Columbia International University) for three years; transferring to Covenant College, a new Presbyterian College in St. Louis, MO from which he graduated with a B.A. in Philosophy. After graduation, he enrolled in Covenant Theological Seminary where he received a B.D. in theology, and returned later for his M.A. He and his wife make their home in Centreville, AL; He has four children; 16 Grandchildren and 14 Great Grandchildren. His other books are available on Amazon.

Realizing Significance, 236 pages, The author summarizes the heart of this book. He explains: "We know about their existence (little people) and some of their needs but we can be so focused on "us", "me", or "I" that we miss seeing or caring for "them", "they" or the "unknown".

Taking A Serious God Seriously, 224 pages, is a clarion call for Christians to return to the standards of Scripture, because God is serious about how Christians should think and live in this world. Every chapter defines what it means to have a serious relationship with a serious God.

The Twenty First Century Church: Is It Waxing Or Waning, 226 pages, This book examines the contemporary church to see if it measures up to the standards of the Bible. It reveals the failure of the church in relationship to the biblical model.

Practical Awareness of Living in the Presence of God, 186 pages, The author wrote this book to give Christians a greater awareness of the Glory of the Lord's Presence in their daily walk and relationship with Him.

Amid the Cultural Chaos: Are We Casualties or Conquerors? 241 pages, Each chapter in this book throws out the gauntlet for Christians to choose a godly culture.

Trending Toward Cultural Captivity: Learning to Survive the Inevitable, 158 pages, This book examines some of the trends that have become overwhelming and a strong influence upon the direction of the nation and world.

Navigating the Cultural Maze: Searching for the Only Way Out, 147 pages, This book will provide you with challenging insights and encouragement to be a light shining into and piercing the darkness in your life.

The Right Course and the Only Right Choice, 154 pages, This book will help Christians gain greater insight in terms of their spiritual journey

The Journey Along the Narrow Way: Jesus Led Me All the Way, 346 pages,

About the Author

[Double Click To Add Text]

www.ingramcontent.com/pod-product-compliance
Lightning Source LLC
Chambersburg PA
CBHW060824050426
42453CB00008B/576